Buns and Burgers

Buns and Burgers

Handcrafted Burgers from Top to Bottom

Gregory Berger

CORAL GABLES

Copyright © 2019 Gregory Berger

Cover Design: Gregory Berger

Layout Design: Jermaine Lau

Published by Mango Publishing Group, a division of Mango Media Inc.

Mango is an active supporter of authors' rights to free speech and artistic expression in their books. The purpose of copyright is to encourage authors to produce exceptional works that enrich our culture and our open society.

Uploading or distributing photos, scans, or any content from this book without prior permission is theft of the author's intellectual property. Please honor the author's work as you would your own. Thank you in advance for respecting our author's rights.

For permission requests, please contact the publisher at:

Mango Publishing Group
2850 Douglas Road, 2nd Floor
Coral Gables, FL 33134 USA
info@mango.bz

Buns and Burgers: Handcrafted Burgers from Top to Bottom

ISBN: (p) 978-1-64250-116-2 (e) 978-1-64250-117-9

LCCN: 2019944141

BISAC: CKB009000—COOKING / Courses & Dishes / Bread

To Lori, the love of my life, who continually inspires me to be my better self and gives me the confidence to look life in the eye and say, "Yeah, I can do this."

To my son Rowan, who brings joy and happiness to our lives each day and isn't afraid of seeds on buns anymore.

TABLE OF CONTENTS

Part 1: Introduction

How to Use This Book	15
Your Tools	17
10 Tips for Baking Buns (In No Particular Order)	21
10 Tips for Cooking the Best Burgers (In No Particular Order)	25
Cook the Burger	27
Bake the Buns	29
Buy It vs. Make It	35

Part 2: Butcher, Farmer, Baker

The Butcher	41
The Farmer	45
The Baker	47

Part 3: Recipes

Sesame Milk Buns	51
The Classic Burger	53
The Easiest Buns	55
Oklahoma Onion Burger	59
Red Sea Salt Buns	60
The Hawaiian Burger	63
Caraway Seed Buns	65
Reuben Burger	67
Green Olive Paprika Buns	69
Lemon Caper Burger	71

Cheddar Jalapeño Potato Buns	75
Cheddar Apple Burger	77
Everything Bagel Seasoning Potato Buns	81
Quinoa Salmon Burger with Avocado Crema	83
Cornflakes Poppy Seed Buns	86
The Golden State Kumquat Burger	88
Black Charcoal Slider Buns	90
Cod Cake Sliders	92
Blue Cheese Poppy Seed Buns	95
Mushroom Swiss Burger	99
Brioche Buttermilk Buns	101
Cubano Burger	105
Peanut Butter Buns	106
The Elvis Burger	109
Soft Pretzel Buns	110
Homemade Nacho Cheese Burger	113
Roasted Red Pepper Buns	117
Bloody Mary Burger	119
Honey Corn Bread Buns	121
Plantain, Forbidden Rice, and Sweet Potato Burger	123
Lemon Green Olive Buns	126
Cauliflower Caper Veggie Burger	128
Poppy Seed Honey Buns	130
White Bean and Pea Shoot Burger	133
Red Beet Buns	136
Aussie Burger	139
Poblano Jack Buns	141
Elote Burger	143

Dutch Crunch Buns	147
Southwest Bean and Corn Burger	149
Popcorn Buns	152
Figs and Honey Burger	155
Lemon Poppy Seed Buns	156
Blueberry Salmon Burger	158
Vegan Whole Wheat Buns	161
Vegan Quinoa Burger with Curry Sauce	162
Leek, Cheddar, and Bacon Waffles	165
Pimento Cheddar Bacon Waffle Burger	167
Green Onion Black Pepper Waffles	169
Black Garlic and Asparagus Waffle Burger	171
Green Onion Pita Bread	173
Greek Pita Burger	175
English Muffins	177
English Muffin "Breakfast for Dinner" Burger	181
Ciabatta Buns	183
Bánh mì Burger	186
Pullman Bread	189
Pullman Patty Melt	192
Mini Cinnamon Buns	194
Ice Cream Dessert Burgers	197
And Finally, the Rowan Berger	199
Acknowledgments	201
About the Author	203w

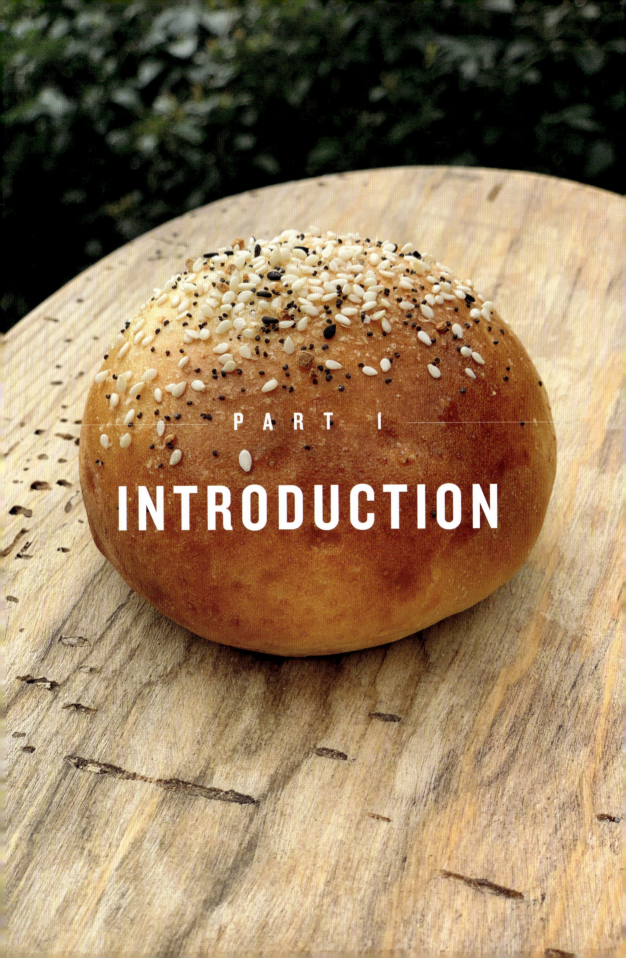

PART I
INTRODUCTION

Sometime in my high school years, back in the early '90s, my family took a summer vacation to New Orleans. This trip, which seemed like it would be an uneventful sightseeing tour, ended up being a life changing adventure. There was gumbo. There was jambalaya. There was étouffée. At one point, the gumbo was accompanied by a full marching band playing "Saints Go Marching In." The flavors of this trip awoke my taste buds, which up to that point were a little bit adventurous, but barely beyond a typical Midwestern kid's palate. (I had tried shrimp but it was fried. I had seen an avocado, but never tasted one, and wouldn't have been able to find the heart of an artichoke if the world depended on it). Bill Knapp's chocolate cakes on birthdays and Marion's Pizza were our equivalent of the French Laundry restaurant.

Soon after that trip, I graduated high school and went to college, where I honed my chicken salad (now with grapes!) and gumbo skills. I moved back home after graduating. That's when the next big, lifechanging thing happened: The Food Network. For real, The Food Network. Before the channel morphed into a bunch of reality shows, there were actual people showing you how to cook actual food! I spent hours watching *Essence of Emeril*, *Too Hot Tamales*, and *Grillin' & Chillin'*. Bobby Flay and Jack McDavid were roasting red peppers on a kettle grill. Emeril Lagasse was blackening shrimp and making a *rémoulade*. Susan Finnegan and Mary Sue Milliken were adding mangos to a salsa. Groundbreaking in my head! I would watch a show, run to the store and buy the ingredients, and then make it that same night for my parents. Nine out of ten times, this was a great success.

After that summer cooking so many delicious meals, I moved to Chicago. I applied to the Culinary Institute, but ultimately decided against it, choosing a day job in graphic design over the kitchen life.

Jump ahead to 2013. The previous fifteen years had been spent making a ton of great food. I'd become a fairly good cook. I read cookbooks, cooking magazines, watched the shows. But in 2013, I came across a copy of Michael Pollan's book *Cooked*. One of the sections was about making sourdough bread. For some reason, this drew me the most. Then I immediately bought Chad Robertson's *Tartine*, and began a baking quest. I collected natural yeast from the air, and pretty soon was producing some very nice loaves.

The loaves got better and better. I started entering them in the California State Fair, and started winning. I started getting offers to buy my bread, to get the recipes, to teach classes. So this is what I did: I started helping local restaurants write recipes

for bread that fit their meal schedules, I started teaching classes here and there, I started doing burger popups with my "Burger-in-law," Rodney.

And now, I want to teach you how to do this. Just as I learned how to cook from watching television and reading books, *you* can learn by reading this book, by seeking out baking shows, and by watching videos on the internet.

Baking and sharing bread has been done for thousands of years, but it seems our culture has forgotten how. There are few things more rewarding than the smell of baking bread and the sight of fresh loaves coming out of the oven. Sure, it'll take some practice. Some of your buns will be misshapen. Sometimes they'll overproof, because you had to go pick up your kid or run to the store, and you got distracted. Sometimes you'll forget to turn on the oven timer, and you'll burn the buns, or your oven will be too hot, and you'll toast the tops to a crisp. Don't worry; it's just flour and a few ingredients. Start over and try again. You'll get it!

HOW TO USE THIS BOOK

I'm often inspired to bake or cook because of an Instagram photo, or a recipe I see while flipping through a book. Most of the time, when I look at a recipe, I only need to grasp the basics and then make it without referring back to the specifics. Or I see a photo and try to recreate a version of what I saw with whatever I have on hand.

Most of the recipes in this book lend themselves to that style of cooking. They are mainly a starting off point or a suggestion. If you can't find pea sprouts, use lettuce. If you have arugula, but the recipe calls for leaf lettuce, go for it! The greens are simply to provide a nice cool crunch, and a break from all the meat and carbs. Also, most of the cheeses in this book are interchangeable. Cheddar, Swiss, manchego, even American, can be used equivalently on just about any burger, should you like one but not another. Or, just use what you already have!

For the beef, try to use a little less, and get the best you can buy. Go to a butcher or grocery store that carries sustainable, grass-fed beef. You can easily make one pound of good beef stretch into four burgers.

A lot of recipes say, "Add salt and pepper to taste." I recommend that you salt everything, and salt often. When cooking, add a little throughout the cooking process, not just at the end. This helps flavor the food from the inside, not just the outside. I keep a small bowl of kosher salt nearby, and I throw in a pinch here and there. Using pinches instead of a shaker helps ensure that you aren't over-salting.

In the baking part of this book, however, you do need to be a little more precise. The measurements and the basic ingredients can be pretty important. You can't just sub almond milk for regular milk, or oil for butter. But the baking part is also a great place to let your creativity shine! Many people will tell you that baking is an exact science, but don't let that intimidate you. Most bakers and baking books use the metric system, digital scales, and ratios to write the recipes. If you seriously get into baking, metric is great! I use a digital scale most of the time. But I wanted this book to be as easy for you as possible, so I stuck with the tried-and-true cups and teaspoons. All the recipes here have been tested, but sometimes I didn't precisely remember the measurements. Did I use exactly a quarter cup of sugar? Did I pack the flour into the cup, or was it spooned in? Don't worry; the recipes will work, regardless. They're just buns.

But there are some things that I do and use that you probably should as well, in order to improve your success. Here's a list of equipment and ingredients that I use when baking and cooking.

Ingredients

Bread Flour

All the recipes in this book use bread flour. It's higher in protein than regular all-purpose flour, so it forms a smoother, tighter bun. It costs a little more, but it's worth it. If you use regular all-purpose or a mix of both, your results may vary.

Eggs

I use Grade A large eggs for all the recipes. Try to use cage free, free range eggs, or better yet, find someone with a chicken. Just note that if you are using eggs from a friend or from your own backyard, they may vary in size, from really small to "Is that a goose egg?"

Seeds & Toppings

You'll save a *lot* of money on things like poppy seed and sesame seed if you can find them in bulk or in an ethnic grocery store. I get a three-pound bag of poppy seeds from a Russian market for less than the cost of a little spice jar at the grocery store. For pretzel salt (which is a must for the salt-topped buns), I find that online.

Milk

For the recipes that use milk, I always use organic one-percent milk. Whole and two percent will also work, and I'm pretty sure that in a pinch, fat-free would work, too. Almond milk will not.

Salt

Kosher salt or sea salt are the only way to go. Ditch the table salt.

Yeast

All the recipes use active dry yeast. Buy a big bag at Costco, then transfer it to a Mason jar, and keep it in the fridge. I use Red Star brand.

Equipment

Stand Mixer

Just about all the recipes can benefit from a stand mixer with a dough hook. If you don't have one, you are going to get really strong arms. You can mix by hand, but the dough hook makes quick work, and you can leave the dough in the mixer bowl for the first rise.

Rimmed Baking Sheets

Get four sixteen-by-twenty-inch rimmed baking sheets. The rim helps keep the little seeds and bits from sliding off the sheets and onto the oven floor.

Pre-Cut Parchment

To go with your new baking sheets, also get pre-cut parchment paper to line them. It makes life easier. I've only ever seen these online.

Dough Scraper

A rectangle dough scraper will help immensely by letting you divide the dough into smaller pieces. It'll also help you get the dough off your cutting board, especially with some of the stickier doughs. I have a cheap plastic one, and it's great.

Pullman Loaf Pan

For the last bread recipe, you'll need a rectangular Pullman loaf pan, found online.

SESAME
POPPY
WHOLE WHEAT
BRIOCHE
POTATO
ENGLISH MUFFIN
SEED
CIBATTA
KAISER
WAFFLE
MILK

10 TIPS FOR BAKING BUNS
(IN NO PARTICULAR ORDER)

1. Start with great ingredients if you want great buns! I almost always use King Arthur or Bob's Red Mill bread flour for all the recipes. Sure, it is a little more expensive, but shop around. I've noticed that some stores charge two or three dollars more a bag than other stores. And if you can, buy locally grown and milled flour. You can also buy in bulk!

2. Get pre-cut parchment paper that matches the size of your baking sheets. I get twelve-by-sixteen-inch pre-cut sheets on Amazon. It saves time and frustration, and because they are flat, they won't roll up on your rolls.

3. Find someone with a chicken, and trade bread for eggs. It'll make you feel good, and you'll be like old-timey barterers.

4. Get good equipment. You don't need top-of-the-line, but get a few nice rimmed baking sheets, the pre-cut parchment, a good dough scraper, and a few brushes for the egg wash. A KitchenAid mixer with a dough hook doesn't hurt, either.

5. Seventy degrees is the optimum kitchen temperature for rising and baking. Too hot, and the buns can proof too quickly. Too cold, and they'll take a lot longer.

6. Midway through the baking, rotate the baking sheets for more even browning.

7. Keep your yeast in the fridge in a big Mason jar. On the shelf, those little packets of yeast can get lost between the Jell-O and the mail. But a big ole Mason jar of yeast says "BAKE US! LET'S DO THIS!" every time you open the fridge.

8. PLAN AHEAD! These buns and breads are relatively easy to make: about 15 minutes to mix and knead, another hour to bulk up, then a few minutes to roll into balls, 2 hours to rise again, and then 20 minutes or so to bake. Easy! But they require uninterrupted blocks of time. You suddenly remember you need to pick up the kids at school…that you need to swing by the bank…and now, mom just called! So try to plan ahead, and make sure that your other responsibilities don't conflict.

9. Be patient. See number 8. Those kinds of things will happen at some point. Sometimes your buns will overproof and deflate. Or they'll underproof, because you had to get them into the oven too soon, and they'll split open funny. Don't give up! Making buns is a skill that's going to take a little practice to master.

10. Bake often! You'll quickly learn what works and what doesn't. You'll soon be able to tell if your dough is too sticky (may need to add a bit more flour), or too firm (thank the yeast for trying and start over). Just don't give up!

    BONUS TIP: Get seed toppings like poppy seeds and sesame seeds at a store with a bulk food section. You'll get a lot more for your bucks, so you can use more, and feel extra generous.

10 TIPS FOR COOKING THE BEST BURGERS
(IN NO PARTICULAR ORDER)

1. Always toast your buns. A little butter and a hot pan or grill will wake up your buns, softening the middles and crispening the bottoms.

2. Don't add stuff to your beef, except salt. (Exception: the James Beard Foundation's Blended Burger Project, try that one.)

3. Always use 80/20 ground beef that you grind yourself, or get from a local butcher or grocery with great sustainability standards.

4. Buy fresh, local, in-season ingredients. I'm writing this book in the early spring, so you are not going to see a ton of tomatoes here, even though I'd love to tell you how great our tomatoes are in Sacramento.

5. Get your "mise" in place. *Mise en place* is a French cooking term for "everything in its place." "*Oh, merde*" means "I can't find the mayo, and now the burgers are getting cold, and the buns are on fire" (or something close to that). Lay out all your burger ingredients before you get started.

6. Big fat burgers are not my favorite. All these recipes use a quarter pound patty. If you want more beef, grill up two and do a double stack, but don't make a giant half pound hockey puck of meat.

7. After cooking the burgers, let them rest on a clean plate for a few minutes to let the juices sink back into the patty, or you're going to soak through your buns.

8. Proper burger construction: bottom bun, then mayo/mustard, then lettuce (which will help form a barrier between juicy beef and bready bun), then the beef, then the rest of the toppings. Lettuce, you have a job to do.

9. Flavor balance. I like to add weird stuff in my burgers, like kumquat jam. But to do this, you also need a salty element to balance it out, like manchego cheese. When mixing flavors, try to always think about sweet, salty, bitter, and sour (you know, how your tongue works!).

MAYO HOT SAUCE BBQ
AIOLI
MUSTARD KETCHUP MARMALADE
PESTO
REMOULADE
RANCH
COMPOTE SPECIAL

COOK THE BURGER

There are a few different ways to properly cook a burger patty. You can pan fry it, grill it, or smash-grill it. But the USDA recommends cooking ground meats to an internal temperature of at least 160 degrees fahrenheit, which means "no pink."

Pan Fry

Take a quarter pound of ground beef, and gently flatten it, being careful not to squish it too much. With your fingers, make a dimple in the center (this will help it cook more evenly). Turn the stovetop on medium, and heat your pan with a little butter or oil. Make sure it's hot before adding the burger. Salt the burger, place in the pan, and listen for the sizzle! Cook for about 5 minutes, then flip. The cooked side should have a nice, dark brown sear. Add your cheese, and cook for another 3 to 5 minutes. Check inside the burger by making a little cut to test the doneness. A little pink is "medium."

Grilling

If using a gas grill, turn the heat up to high and wait. If using a charcoal grill, heat the coals and wait until they have turned orange and have ashed-over. Brush the burgers with oil, and generously salt them. Grill the burgers until they are browned and starting to char up a bit, about 3 minutes, depending on how hot your coals are. Flip over the burgers, add cheese, and cook until the desired doneness.

Smash Burger-ing

I find this is best done outside, because you'll get a bunch of splattered oil and smoke, but it's worth it! Get a heavy bottomed pan, cast iron is ideal. If doing it outside, a baking steel or a cast iron *plancha* is great. Either way, heat it to piping hot. Take a quarter pound of beef, and lightly pack it into a ball. Season the ball with salt and pepper. Place the ball on the smoking hot surface, and then smash it down with a heavy spatula (my friend Rodney uses a metal tile trowel he got at a hardware store) and hold it down for about 2 minutes. Then, using the spatula or trowel, scrape up the burger (including all the good, crackly bits) and flip. Add cheese and cook about a minute longer.

BAKE THE BUNS

Here is a step-by-step guide for making perfect buns. It uses the Easiest Buns recipe on page 61.

1. In the mixer bowl, add the flour, sugar, salt, yeast, egg, butter, and warm water. Stick your finger in it to make sure it's not too hot, because you don't want to kill the yeast.
2. Add the dough hook, and mix on medium for about 5 to 6 minutes.
3. After a few minutes, the dough should start coming together in one or more balls.
4. Remove the hook, and use your hands to combine the dough into one ball, and cover the bowl with a towel for an hour.
5. Look, it's twice as big as it was!

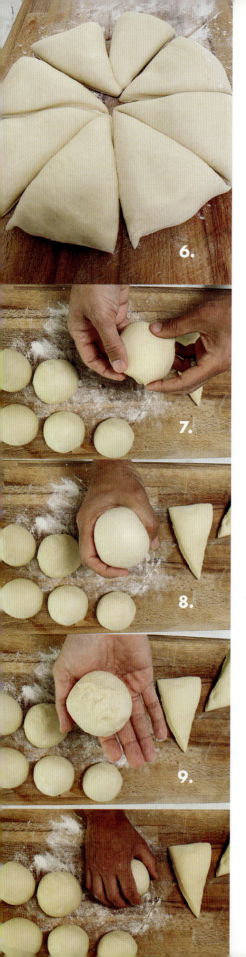

6. Turn out the dough onto a cutting board. With a dough scraper, cut the ball into eight equal pieces, like a pizza.

7. Line two sheet pans with parchment. Take each dough triangle in your palm, and make a ball with it.

8. Make an "OK" sign with your fingers, and push the ball up through the hole in the "OK", so that the top of the ball gets stretched smooth. Then pinch the bottom of the ball to seal it.

9. Now, on your cutting board or other work surface, place a dough ball seam-down, cupping your hand in contact with the top. Quickly roll the ball inside your cupped hand a few times to finish the shaping. Do all eight like this.

10. Place the balls on the baking sheets a few inches apart from each other. Cover and let rise for 1.5 to 2 hours.

11. Now they have risen again to about twice their original size. Preheat oven to 375 degrees.

12. Mix an egg yolk with a few drops of water, and using a brush, paint the tops of each ball with the mixture. Cover the whole top, but don't worry about the sides, because drips are fine! Then sprinkle the tops with seeds. Be generous!

13. Bake for 10 minutes, and rotate the sheets. Bake for 8 to 10 more minutes.

14. You've got buns! Eat them today, or store in a plastic bag for 2 to 3 days. You can also freeze them!

ICEBERG
ROMAINE
DANDELION
LEAF LEAF
FRISÉE
BUTTER
SPINACH
BIBB
ENDIVE
KALE
ARUGULA

BUY IT VS. MAKE IT

Buns: Uh…

Ketchup: Buy it. You don't need to use ketchup, but if you must, there's really only one ketchup that you should buy.

Mayo: This one is tricky. Homemade mayonnaise is great, but so is mayo in a jar. If you are worried about using raw eggs in homemade, then buy mayo from the store. But if you have access to fresh organic eggs, try homemade.

Pickles: Tie. There are plenty of great pickles on your store shelf. Some of them, like sweet little gherkins, are hard to make, because you may not be able to get the right kind of cucumber, unless you grow them yourself. But dill pickles, that's another story. They are easy to make, and you can find perfect sized pickling cucumbers and fresh dill at your farmers market. And the Quick Pickle recipe in this book is super easy!

Mustard: Tie. Mustard from the store usually contains the same few ingredients that you'd use at home. But making it is also fun.

American cheese: Buy. For this book, I tried to make homemade American cheese. No good.

Ground beef: Buy. I don't grind meat. I just don't. I let Eric the Butcher do that. You can grind it yourself if you want 100 percent control of what goes into the burgers, but if you know your butcher, you can trust that they'll do it right.

Veggie burgers: Make. 100 percent. Veggie burgers are great! Making them at home will get you 100 percent real ingredients, with no weird fillers.

IMMERSION BLENDER MAYO

- 1 cup avocado oil
- 1 large egg (fresh, organic, room temperature)
- 1 teaspoon lemon juice
- ½ teaspoon Dijon mustard
- ¼ teaspoon salt

Place all ingredients in a jar or cup. Insert the stand mixer, and mix on high for about a minute. Then slowly move the mixer up and down, until it's all white and looks like mayo! (About another minute or two.) Refrigerate until ready to use. Will keep for about two weeks.

REFRIGERATOR DILLS

- 4 pickling cucumbers
- 8 sprigs fresh dill
- 4 garlic cloves, peeled but kept whole
- 4 teaspoons black peppercorns
- 4 teaspoons coriander seed

FOR THE BRINE

- 2 cups water
- 4 tablespoons white vinegar
- 2 teaspoons kosher salt (or pickling salt)

Cut the cucumbers into round slices or spears. Divide the dill, garlic, peppercorns, and coriander seed between two clean pint jars. Then pack as much cut cucumber into the jars as possible.

In a pot, bring the water, vinegar, and salt to a boil. Remove from heat. Carefully pour this brine mixture over the cucumber and fill each jar. Screw on the lids, and put in fridge for a day or two before using. They will keep like this for a few months.

DIJON-STYLE MUSTARD

- ½ cup mustard seeds, a combination of brown and yellow
- ½ cup white wine
- ½ cup white wine vinegar
- ½ teaspoon kosher salt
- 1 tablespoon honey

In a small bowl, mix everything except the honey, and let it sit for about 24 hours.

The next day, add the honey, and mix in a blender. Put it in a lidded jar, and keep in your fridge for a day or two before using. The mustard will stay good until you eat it all.

PART 2

BUTCHER, FARMER, BAKER

THE BUTCHER

Peas and carrots, Forrest and Jenny, peanut butter and jelly, and most importantly, Burgers and Buns. All legendary couples.

Simply put, if you begin with a great patty, and use a fresh homemade bun, you can stop there. With nothing else, you're already a winner. Taking the burger further to legendary status is easy after you have the two key components.

I am a butcher. I'll stick to the meaty parts and leave the bun part to Greg. He's a bread wizard.

There are as many opinions on what makes a great burger patty as there are leaves on a tree. I think it comes down to three key factors: source, fat content, and grind.

I source grass-fed and finished beef for my burgers. It makes me feel good knowing the animal was naturally fed and had a pretty good life. No hormones, antibiotics, or any of that other stuff I don't want to eat. Besides, grass fed and finished beef (no feed lot, no grain) has an amazing flavor. When you start with great beef, there's really no need to jazz it up with anything other than salt and pepper. Like a ripe tomato, they're delicious as-is, whereas a tomato in winter is going to need serious work even to get it to "OK."

Fat content controls the flavor and juice of a burger. Simply put, if a grind is too lean (90 percent or more), a burger will taste dry, tough, and pretty bland. A grind that is too fatty (30 percent or more), will eat greasy, and good luck trying to cook these on a grill. (Good-bye eyebrows.) At my butcher shop, V. Miller Meats (shameless plug), we shoot for 80/20. This allows the burgers to be flavorful, cook easily, and taste great. We start the blend with about 50 percent chuck for a good base (chuck is naturally about 25 percent fat), and add various trimmings from the morning butchery action. This usually includes sirloin (lean), rib eye (fatty), and other delicious bits from all over the animal—always shooting for that 80/20 percentage.

The grind and patty processes are overlooked all too often. I have very few absolutes in my world, but one of them is grinding beef only once. This allows for the burger to still have a meaty texture, and for the fat to cook into the burger, and not fireball on the grill. One way you can tell if your beef has been ground more than once is to ask. Butchers love to chat about this stuff. What's in the grind today (remember fat content)? When was this ground (freshness counts)? How many times was it ground? If more than once, it tells me the fat is likely to break out when I cook the burger. If the butcher seems disturbed or annoyed by your questions, maybe go looking for a new butcher. When making the patty, I find a ring mold works great. I put down parchment paper and lightly pat the beef into the mold. Lightly packing the meat makes a little more delicate patty, and gives a great meaty mouth-feel to your burger.

I hope this helps. I hope you dig this book. Greg has been a great partner in crime on many meaty top-secret projects, and you've never seen a bunch of butchers swoon like when he comes into the shop with a batch of "tester buns."

Eric V. Miller

V. Miller Meats Craft Butchery

THE FARMER

To me, organic farming is not just a method of growing fruits and vegetables, but is more like a way of life, dedicated to preserving and protecting our agricultural lands, enriching our understanding of natural biological processes, and creating a more vibrant community centered around the food we eat every day.

The true meaning of organic agriculture begins and ends with the health of our soil. The earth has, over millennia, provided us with all the nutrients and minerals we need to grow spectacular produce, and, as an organic farmer, it is my job to preserve the biological processes already present in the soil, so that we can enjoy the bounty of the harvest for generations to come.

By avoiding pesticides, herbicides, and other chemicals, I can allow the hardy ecosystem of earthworms, good bacteria, and other parts of our living soil to thrive and work their magic in giving us delicious crops to enjoy at our dinner tables. Several techniques, including good crop rotation, well-timed plantings, minimal tillage, cover cropping, efficient irrigation, and the incorporation of organic compost into the soil, all contribute to building a robust organic farming system.

One of the most essential aspects of being a farmer is the opportunity to help foster community around the food we provide. So while we build our soil, we also share the fruits of our labor with all our friends and neighbors at our local farmers' market. If I can introduce a customer to vegetables they have never tried before, and get them to take those vegetables home to their families, where they cook new meals, share different tastes, trade stories, and create stronger bonds over the food I produce, it makes the hard work, effort, and dedication I've put into becoming a good farmer all worthwhile.

Jay Cuff

Hearty Fork Farm

THE BAKER

"There is no chiropractic treatment, no Yoga exercise, no hour of meditation in a music-throbbing chapel, that will leave you emptier of bad thoughts than this homely ceremony of making bread."

—M.F.K. Fisher, *The Art of Eating*

I still don't really identify myself as a baker, even though there are a lot of folks that only know me as a baker. I still say "graphic designer" when someone asks what I do. But what I really *do* is bake. I bake all the time. I bake loaves, I bake buns, I bake English muffins. There is always a loaf either on its way, or noodling around in my brain, trying to get out. But I don't work in a bakery, and I never have. I did plenty of time in a kitchen, but never in a real, working bakery.

Baking allows me time to breathe each day I do it. It gives me a break from the bustle of getting my kid to school, packing lunches, answering emails and texts, plus cramming in a full day of work. Baking has little moments built into the process that force you to take a break. It's been an hour—time to punch down the dough. It's doubled in size—time to roll the buns. It's rested for 20 minutes—time for the salt. These little moments bring me out of my head and my regular work life, and force me to be present, even just for a few minutes.

There's a magic to taking a few ingredients, mixing and kneading, and turning them into a work of art. I think it's important to know how to make and serve your friends and family the bread that came from your own hands, and was baked in your own oven. No thiamin mononitrate. No soy lecithin. Riboflavin? Nope. So, it's going to get moldy more quickly. It's going to dry out after a few days. But those are good things! It's scarier to see a loaf of bread that doesn't get moldy. I'll take the mold.

Another thing baking does is that it allows one to make connections that might not have happened without bread. I bake so much that my little family couldn't possibly eat all that I make, so I give it away. I call it "bread bombing," and it's the best. Think of it as a "ding dong ditch," but instead, you leave a loaf of fresh sourdough. I think that sharing food, especially something you created, is one of the most rewarding things you can do. It fills my cup, and fills someone else with bread.

Baking at home has earned me access to a life I thought I always wanted, but for which I never pulled the trigger: the kitchen life. I now get to go behind the scenes at some of my favorite restaurants, go into food trucks, and instead of just ordering from the window I get to be behind the curtain doing the work, and not just doing the eating. It it never just about the eating, it's about the life of hot pans, flaming grills, boiling pots, knives flashing, and plates flying. I get to work back there now, but only for a bit, until I go back home, to my quiet life of dogs, kids, my wife, emails, packing lunches and…breathing.

I know I am a baker.

GREGORY BERGER

Baker

PART 3
RECIPES

SESAME MILK BUNS

These are soft super-flavorful buns. The extra step at the beginning is almost like making a roux. It adds tenderness to the buns. The sesame seed is traditional, but you can top with whatever you want!

Prep time: 20 minutes, plus about 1.5 hours to proof

Cook time: 25–30 minutes

Makes 8 buns

To Make This Bun

- ⅓ cup bread flour
- ¾ cup water
- 2½ cups bread flour
- 1 tablespoon white sugar
- 2 teaspoons yeast
- 1 teaspoon sea salt
- 1 egg
- ½ cup milk
- ¼ cup softened butter
- 1 egg yolk (for egg wash)
- 2 tablespoons sesame seed

In a small saucepan over medium heat, whisk together the smaller amount of bread flour and the water (the first two ingredients), until they turn into a smooth, thick paste. Let cool for a bit.

Get out your electric mixer with a dough hook. Mix together the next four dry ingredients in the mixer bowl. In a separate bowl, whisk the egg and milk together. On low speed, slowly add the egg/milk mixture, then add the paste you made earlier.

Mix on medium speed for 5 minutes. Then break apart the softened butter into clumps, and toss into the running mixer. Mix for an additional 3 minutes. The dough will look smooth, but will be super sticky.

Scoop the dough into a lightly oiled bowl. Move the dough ball around until it's oiled all over. Then cover with a towel for about an hour.

When dough is big and puffy, it's time to make the buns. Dump the dough onto a cutting board. It'll deflate, but don't worry, that yeast is still working for you. Divide the dough into eight pieces. Do your best to roll each piece of sticky dough into a smooth ball. It helps to fold the dough over itself, so that the top side of the ball has a tight smooth surface.

Preheat oven to 325 degrees.

Place the dough balls on two parchment lined baking sheets, four per sheet. (This is just for looks. I like a bun that hasn't baked in contact with another bun. You can space them all out on one sheet, but they may rise into each other.) Lightly brush each ball with egg yolk (mix a yolk with a few drops of water), then generously sprinkle with sesame seed. Let rise for about 20 minutes.

Bake for 25–30 minutes or until the tops start to brown. Let cool on wire racks.

THE CLASSIC BURGER

This is it, the quintessential burger. It's the burger to represent all burgers. It's the burger you get when you draw a picture of a burger. It's the burger you see when you dream of them. It's what a fast food burger strives to be, and what a backyard burger can become (if you follow the rules). Fresh, quality ingredients are important, especially the tomatoes. Remember, nothing can beat a homegrown tomato. The Special Sauce isn't really that special, it's mainly a mix of the traditional condiments you'd be likely to put on your burger, but blended all together.

Prep time:
25 minutes to cook and assemble

Makes 4 burgers

To Make This Burger

- 1 pound ground beef
- Special Sauce
- 4 slices American cheese
- Fresh onions
- Fresh tomato
- Leaf or iceberg lettuce
- Pickles
- Salt and pepper
- Sesame Seed Buns

Divide the beef into four equal patties, and generously salt and pepper. In pan or on grill, cook them for about 4 to 5 minutes, then flip for another 2 to 3 minutes. Add a slice of American cheese, and melt.

Cut your buns, and butter and toast them.

Starting with the bottom bun, add a smear of Special Sauce, the lettuce, and then the onions and tomato. Then add the burger patty with the cheese, the pickles, and finally the top bun.

SPECIAL SAUCE

- ½ cup mayo
- 3 tablespoons ketchup
- 2 tablespoons sweet pickle relish
- 1 ½ teaspoons sugar
- 1 ½ teaspoons distilled white vinegar

Mix all together, and chill for a bit to let the flavors meld.

THE EASIEST BUNS

Like the name says, these are the easiest buns in the book! Put seven ingredients in a bowl, mix for a bit, rest, roll the balls, rest, brush with egg wash, bake, and boom! Buns! Master this recipe and the others will come easily, because this is the mother recipe for a lot of the buns in this book.

Prep time:
30 minutes, plus about 2.5 hours to proof

Cook time:
15-18 minutes

Makes 8 buns

To Make This Bun

- 1 cup lukewarm water
- 2 tablespoons unsalted butter, cold, cut into pieces
- 1 large egg
- 3½ cups bread flour
- ¼ cup sugar
- 1¼ teaspoons salt
- 2 teaspoons active dry yeast
- 1 egg yolk (for egg wash)

In the mixer bowl, stir everything together, except the egg yolk for the wash. Mix with the dough hook for about 5 minutes or until the dough forms one or more smooth balls.

If there are several balls, use your hands to combine. Cover with a towel for about 1 hour or until doubled in size.

Divide the dough into eight pieces. Do your best to roll each piece into a smooth ball. It helps to fold the dough over itself so that the top side of the ball becomes a tight smooth surface. Make sure you place it seam side down on the parchment.

Place the balls on two parchment-lined baking sheets, four per sheet. Lightly cover, and let rise for about 1.5 hours or until very puffy.

Preheat oven to 375 degrees.

Lightly brush each bun with egg yolk (mix a yolk with a few drops of water). Add any seeds at this point, or leave them off.

Bake for about 15–18 minutes or until golden brown. Let cool on wire racks.

CHEROKEE PURPLE
BRANDYWINE
SAN MARZANO
GREEN ZEBRA
CHERRY
BEEFSTEAK
SUNGOLD
ROMA
SWEET 100
EARLY GIRL

OKLAHOMA ONION BURGER

I had never heard of this style burger until a local restaurant, Empress Tavern, offered it for lunch a few months ago. It didn't sound like something I would love. Yet I understand the appeal of American cheese. It melts really well, and evokes a nostalgia for the homemade grilled cheese sandwiches of childhood. Unfortunately, it's also a super-processed product. But it works really well here! Also, I'm usually not a huge fan of a lot of onion, yet this burger is "all onion"! So if you mix together a ton of onions and some melty processed cheese, what you get is one of the best, simplest burgers in this book.

Prep time:
25 minutes to cook and assemble

Makes 4 burgers

To Make This Burger

- 1 pound ground beef
- 1 large onion, peeled and thinly sliced
- American cheese
- Pickles
- Yellow mustard
- Salt and pepper
- The Easiest Buns

Divide the beef into four equal patties, and generously salt and pepper. In a hot pan, smash down the beef patty, and let cook for a minute. Lay the raw onions on top, and smash them into the meat. Flip the burger, so the onions are now on the bottom, and top with a slice of American cheese. Cook the whole thing for about 2 to 3 more minutes, until the cheese is melted, and the onions are glossy and softening. Slit the buns, and place them in the pan so they can steam and soften.

Starting with the bottom bun, add the burger patty with melted cheese and onion, then a few pickles and a squirt of mustard, and finally the top bun.

RED SEA SALT BUNS

Beautiful buns with a crunchy rose-colored topping, these buns can be used just about anywhere, but are particularly good with the Hawaiian burger.

Prep time:
30 minutes, plus about 2.5 hours to proof

Cook time:
15-18 minutes

Makes 8 buns

To Make This Bun

- 1 cup lukewarm water
- 2 tablespoons unsalted butter, cold, cut into pieces
- 1 large egg
- 3½ cups bread flour
- ¼ cup sugar
- 1¼ teaspoons red sea salt
- 2 teaspoons active dry yeast
- 1 egg yolk (for egg wash)
- Red sea salt for topping

In the mixer bowl, stir everything together except the egg yolk for the wash. Mix with the dough hook for about 5 minutes or until the dough forms one or more smooth balls.

If there are several balls, use your hands to combine. Cover with a towel for about 1 hour or until doubled in size.

Divide the dough into eight pieces. Do your best to roll each piece into a smooth ball. It helps to fold the dough over itself so that the top side of the ball becomes a tight smooth surface. Make sure you place it seam side down on the parchment.

Place the balls on two parchment lined baking sheets, four per sheet. Lightly cover and let rise for about 1.5 hours or until very puffy.

Preheat oven to 375 degrees.

Lightly brush each bun with egg yolk (mix a yolk with a few drops of water). Add red sea salt, or leave them without.

Bake for about 15–18 minutes or until golden brown. Let cool on wire racks.

THE HAWAIIAN BURGER

This claim is surely going to trigger some of you, but I think pineapple is the best pizza topping. It's also great on a burger. On a recent vacation to Kauai, I actually met a family that harvested Hawaiian Red Salt. They gave me a little bag of it, which I had been saving, until I found a use for it. It tastes like good sea salt, but has a beautiful rose color, and irregular shaped flakes. Then it dawned on me that it would be the perfect topper for this burger. If you can't find the red salt, any flaky sea salt will do. Black salt would also look great. With the teriyaki and pineapple, this is a fairly sweet burger, so the salty crunch really adds a nice balance.

Prep time:
25 minutes to cook and assemble

Makes 4 burgers

To Make This Burger

- 1 pound ground beef
- Teriyaki Sauce
- Leaf lettuce
- White cheddar cheese
- 4 pineapple rings (fresh if possible, but not the end of the world if canned)
- Caramelized onion
- Mayo
- Salt and pepper
- Red Sea Salt Buns

Divide the beef into four equal patties, and generously salt and pepper. In pan or on grill, cook them for about 4 to 5 minutes, then flip for another 2 to 3 minutes. Add the cheese after the first flip.

Cut your buns, and butter and toast them.

In a buttered sauté pan or on a grill, sear the pineapple for a few minutes, until the edges start to brown.

Starting with the bottom bun, add a smear of mayo, the lettuce, and the burger patty. Then add the Teriyaki Sauce, a ring of pineapple, a bit of caramelized onion, and finally add the top bun. Umbrellas for garnish, if you have them, or add a little wedge of fresh pineapple.

TERIYAKI SAUCE

- 1 cup water
- 4 tablespoons packed brown sugar
- ¼ cup soy sauce
- 2 tablespoons honey
- 1 large clove of garlic, finely minced
- 2 tablespoons cornstarch
- ¼ cup cold water

Mix the first five ingredients over medium heat. Cook until hot, about 1 minute. Mix the cold water and cornstarch to make a thickener. Add to the pot. Cook and stir until thickened, 5 to 7 minutes.

CARAWAY SEED BUNS

The goal here was to create a rye bun that would still rise like a regular bun. I added just enough rye flour and caraway to get that rye flavor, while keeping the softness of a tradition bun.

Prep time:
30 minutes, plus about 2.5 hours to proof

Cook time:
15-18 minutes

Makes 8 buns

To Make This Bun

- 1 cup lukewarm water
- 2 tablespoons unsalted butter, cold, cut into pieces
- 1 large egg
- 2½ cups bread flour
- 1 cup rye flour
- ¼ cup sugar
- 1¼ teaspoons salt
- 2 teaspoons active dry yeast
- 2 tablespoons caraway seed
- 1 egg yolk (for egg wash)

In the mixer bowl, stir everything together except the egg yolk for the wash. Mix with the dough hook for about 5 minutes or until the dough forms one or more smooth balls.

If there are several balls, use your hands to combine. Cover with a towel for about 1 hour or until doubled in size.

Divide the dough into eight pieces. Do your best to roll each piece into a smooth ball. It helps to fold the dough over itself so that the top side of the ball becomes a tight smooth surface. Make sure you place it seam side down on the parchment.

Preheat oven to 375 degrees.

Place the balls on two parchment lined baking sheets, four per sheet. Lightly cover and let rise for about 1.5 hours or until very puffy.

Lightly brush each bun with egg yolk (mix a yolk with a few drops of water). Add any seeds, or leave them off.

Bake for about 15–18 minutes or until golden brown. Let cool on wire racks.

REUBEN BURGER

A traditional Reuben has corned beef, Russian dressing, and rye bread, but I generally don't like to add extra heavy meats to the burgers, because I like the beef burger flavor to still shine through. I also think Thousand Island tastes better than Russian, but by all means, this is your burger, so you do you. However, the Swiss and sauerkraut better stay, because they really make this burger. The Caraway Seed Buns add a subtle rye flavor, while still having a soft texture.

Prep time:
15 minutes to cook and assemble

Makes 4 burgers

To Make This Burger

- 1 pound ground beef
- Swiss cheese
- Sauerkraut
- Thousand Island dressing
- Dill pickle spears
- Mayo
- Salt and pepper
- Caraway Seed Buns

Divide the beef into four equal patties, and generously salt and pepper. In pan or on grill, cook them for about 4 to 5 minutes, then flip for another 2 to 3 minutes, and add a slice of Swiss cheese. When the cheese is melted, remove the patties.

Cut your buns, and butter and toast them.

Starting with the bottom bun, add mayo, then the burger patty with melted cheese, then a scoop of sauerkraut, the pickles and Thousand Island dressing, and finally the top bun. Extra pickles are always welcome.

GREEN OLIVE PAPRIKA BUNS

Briny green onions dot the interior of these buns, and the paprika adds a spicy sweetness. I think smoked paprika always beats regular paprika, but either can work here! You can use olives with or without the pimentos.

Prep time:
30 minutes, plus about 2.5 hours to proof

Cook time:
15-18 minutes

Makes 8 buns

To Make This Bun

- 1 cup lukewarm water
- 2 tablespoons unsalted butter, cold, cut into pieces
- 1 large egg
- 3½ cups bread flour
- ¼ cup sugar
- 1¼ teaspoons salt
- 2 teaspoons active dry yeast
- 1 cup chopped green olives
- 1 egg yolk (for egg wash)
- 2 teaspoons smoked paprika

In the mixer bowl, stir everything together except the egg yolk for the wash. Mix with the dough hook for about 5 minutes or until the dough forms one or more smooth balls.

If there are several balls, use your hands to combine. Cover with a towel for about 1 hour or until doubled in size.

Divide the dough into eight pieces. Do your best to roll each piece into a smooth ball It helps to fold the dough over itself so that the top side of the ball becomes a tight smooth surface. Make sure you place it seam side down on the parchment.

Preheat oven to 375 degrees.

Place the balls on two parchment-lined baking sheets, four per sheet. Lightly cover and let rise for about 1.5 hours or until very puffy.

Whisk together the egg yolk, paprika, and a few drops of water. Lightly brush each bun with the egg yolk mix.

Bake for about 15 to 18 minutes or until golden brown. Let cool on wire racks.

LEMON CAPER BURGER

Each February and March in California, Meyer lemons become the zucchinis of spring. One tree can produce over ten million lemons. No, that's not true, but they do produce a lot. Bags of them left on doorstops. Lemons tossed into neighbors' yards. Lemons as teacher thank-you gifts. Everyone says to juice them, and make lemon juice cubes or *limoncello*. That's a lot of work, and if you've gotten this far, you are already committed to baking buns. So how about chopping some whole Meyer lemons to make a wonderful burger condiment?

Prep time:
25 minutes to cook and assemble, plus a few hours to chill the relish

Makes 4 burgers

To Make This Burger

- 1 pound ground beef
- 4 tablespoons Lemon Caper Relish
- Leaf lettuce
- Thin shavings of manchego cheese
- Thin slices of Meyer lemon
- Mayo
- Salt and pepper
- Green Olive Paprika Buns

Divide the beef into four equal patties, and generously salt and pepper. In pan or on grill, cook them for about 2 to 3 minutes, then flip for another 2 to 3 minutes.

Cut your buns, and butter and toast them.

Starting with the bottom bun, add a smear of mayo, the lettuce, then the burger patty, then the manchego cheese (don't melt it—in this case it's better if it's not melty), then a few lemon slices, a tablespoon of relish, and finally the top bun. For garnish, spear a few leftover olives with a toothpick.

LEMON CAPER RELISH

- 2 Meyer lemons, seeded and chopped (rind and all)
- 2 tablespoons capers
- 1 tablespoon chopped parsley
- 1 tablespoon good olive oil

Mix and refrigerate for a few hours so the flavors can meld. Will keep in a Mason jar for a few weeks.

CHEDDAR JALAPEÑO POTATO BUNS

These buns were inspired by those bagels topped with jalapeños and cheddar. The cheese inside the bun melts away, but the flavor remains.

Prep time: 30 minutes, plus about 1.5 hours to proof

Cook time: 15-18 minutes

Makes 8 buns

To Make This Bun

- 1 pound russet potatoes, peeled and chopped
- ½ cup shredded cheddar cheese
- 2 tablespoons unsalted butter
- 2 ¼ cups bread flour
- 1 tablespoon sugar
- 2 teaspoons instant yeast
- 1 teaspoon salt
- 5 tablespoons reserved potato water
- 1 egg
- 1 egg yolk (for egg wash)
- 2 tablespoons shredded cheese
- 2 tablespoons chopped pickled jalapeños

Boil the potatoes until cooked through and soft. Reserve 5 tablespoons of potato water for later. Pour out remaining water, then mash the potato until smooth. Add the butter to the warm potato mash, cover, and set aside.

In the mixer bowl, stir together flour, sugar, yeast, and salt. Add the warm potatoes, 1 egg, and the reserved potato water. Mix on low for about 8 to 10 minutes, until the dough is nice and smooth, and just a little bit sticky.

Scoop the dough into a lightly oiled bowl. Move the dough ball around until it's oiled all over. Then cover with a towel for about 30 minutes or until doubled in size.

Do your best to roll each piece of sticky dough into a smooth ball. It helps to fold the dough over itself, so that the top side of the ball has a tight smooth surface.

Preheat oven to 425 degrees.

Place the balls on two parchment lined baking sheets, four per sheet. Lightly cover and let rise for about an hour.

Lightly brush each bun with egg yolk (mix a yolk with a few drops of water), then sprinkle with jalapeños and cheddar.

Bake for about 15 to 18 minutes or until golden brown. Let cool on wire racks.

CHEDDAR APPLE BURGER

This burger makes me think of fall, when the air and the apples are both crisp. Don't leave out the onions. They are worth every second they take to make, and you can't replace the sweet, mellow onion flavor that they add. For the barbecue sauce, I always use a good, store-bought variety. Half of barbecue sauce is ketchup, so whenever I make my own, it feels like I'm just adding stuff to ketchup.

Prep time:
15 minutes to cook and assemble, 3 years or so to caramelize the onions

Makes 4 burgers

To Make This Burger

- 1 pound ground beef
- Caramelized onions
- 4 slices cheddar cheese
- Barbecue sauce
- One big tasty apple, thinly sliced (whatever apple is the best locally)
- Mayo
- Salt and pepper
- Cheddar Jalapeño Potato Buns

Divide the beef into four equal patties, and generously salt and pepper. In pan or on grill, cook them for about 4 to 5 minutes, then flip for another 2 to 3 minutes, then melt the cheddar slice on top of each. Cut your buns and toast them.

Starting with the bottom bun, add a smear of mayo, a few slices of apple, then the burger patty with the melted cheddar. Top that with caramelized onions, barbecue sauce, and finally the top bun.

CARAMELIZED ONIONS

- 1 big onion (any type other than red)
- Salt
- Olive oil

Thinly slice the onions, trying not to cry or chop a finger. Use a pan that you don't mind smelling like onions for the next few times you use it. Heat about a tablespoon of oil, and add the onions. Gently coat them with oil, and toss with a little salt. On low heat, cook the onions until they are about a quarter the amount you started with, and are glossy golden brown. This should take approximately three years of your life. Seriously, it'll take forever. Or at least an hour. Ok, several minutes. Stir them every once in a while, because you don't want them to burn or to brown too quickly. This very gradual cooking will pay off in the end!

EVERYTHING BAGEL SEASONING POTATO BUNS

Everything Bagel Seasoning could be the greatest topping mix ever created. I just buy mine in a shaker, already made, but you can make your own by mixing equal parts regular poppy seed, white sesame seed, black sesame seed, dried minced garlic, dried minced onion, and coarse sea salt.

Prep time:
30 minutes, plus about 1.5 hours to proof

Cook time:
15-18 minutes

Makes 8 buns

To Make This Bun

- 1 pound russet potatoes, peeled and chopped
- 2 tablespoons unsalted butter
- 2¼ cups bread flour
- 1 tablespoons sugar
- 2 teaspoons instant yeast
- 1 teaspoon salt
- 5 tablespoons reserved potato water
- 1 egg
- 1 egg yolk (for egg wash)
- 1 tablespoon Everything Bagel Seasoning

Boil the potatoes until cooked through and soft. Reserve 5 tablespoons of potato water for later. Pour out remaining water, then mash the potato until smooth. Add the butter to the warm potato mash, cover, and set aside.

In the mixer bowl, stir together flour, sugar, yeast, and salt. Add the warm potatoes, 1 egg, and the reserved potato water. Mix on low for about 8 to 10 minutes, until the dough is nice and smooth, and just a little bit sticky.

Scoop the dough into a lightly oiled bowl. Move the dough ball around until it's oiled all over. Then cover with a towel for about 30 minutes or until doubled in size.

Divide the dough into eight pieces. Do your best to roll each piece of sticky dough into a smooth ball. It helps to fold the dough over itself, so that the top side of the ball has a tight smooth surface.

Preheat oven to 425 degrees.

Place the balls on two parchment lined baking sheets, four per sheet. Lightly cover and let rise for about 30 more minutes.

Lightly brush each ball with egg yolk (mix a yolk with a few drops of water), then sprinkle them with the Everything Bagel Seasoning.

Bake for about 15 to 18 minutes or until golden brown. Let cool on wire racks.

QUINOA SALMON BURGER WITH AVOCADO CREMA

This is a super-healthy burger, loaded with good proteins and omegas. Always try to buy wild salmon, not farm raised. I get a subscription box of frozen wild salmon delivered each month, and it makes life so much easier knowing those filets are sitting in the freezer, just waiting to become burgers.

Prep time:
15 minutes to cook and assemble, cook the quinoa and salmon firsts

Makes 4 burgers

To Make This Burger

- 4 Quinoa Salmon Burgers
- Avocado Crema
- Pickled jalapeños (or pickled red onions)
- Watercress (or arugula, or any other tender greens)
- Salt and pepper
- Everything Bagel Buns

Cook your salmon "burgers."

Cut your buns, and toast them in a lightly oiled pan.

Place the salmon patty on the bottom bun, add a generous bloop of crema, add the pickled jalapeños and watercress, and finally the top bun.

QUINOA SALMON BURGER

- 1 cup cooked quinoa
- ¾ cups baked salmon
- ½ cup cooked chopped broccoli
- ½ cup breadcrumbs
- 2 eggs
- Salt & pepper to taste

For the burger: mix all ingredients. Form into four equal balls, then refrigerate for about 20 minutes. Heat a frying pan with butter or oil. When hot, add the four balls, and gently squash down each of them. Cook on medium heat for about 8 minutes per side or until nicely browned. If they fall apart, and there's a great chance they will, try to squish them back into the general patty shape.

AVOCADO CREMA

- 1 ripe avocado
- ¾ cup plain Greek yogurt
- Juice from one lime
- 1 teaspoon salt

In a bowl, mix all the ingredients until smooth, or in a blender, if you want it super smooth.

CORNFLAKES POPPY SEED BUNS

I wanted to make a bun that had corn flavor, but not necessarily a corn bread flavor. Did that make sense?

I did some experiments (Corn Pops were too sweet), and came up with cornflakes as a replacement for some of the flour. This bun is a little denser and sturdier, but also has a surprisingly nice little crunch.

Prep time:
30 minutes, plus about 2.5 hours to proof

Cook time:
15-18 minutes

Makes 8 buns

To Make This Bun

- 1 cup lukewarm water
- 2 tablespoons unsalted butter, cold, cut into pieces
- 1 large egg
- 2½ cups bread flour
- 1 cup crushed cornflakes
- 2 tablespoons poppy seed ¼ cup sugar
- 1¼ teaspoons salt
- 2 teaspoons active dry yeast
- 1 egg yolk (for egg wash)
- 2 tablespoons crushed cornflakes

In the mixer bowl, stir everything together except the egg yolk for the wash, and the extra 2 tablespoons of cornflakes. Mix with the dough hook for about 5 minutes or until the dough forms one or more smooth balls.

If there are several balls, use your hands to combine. Cover with a towel for about 1 hour or until doubled in size.

Divide the dough into eight pieces. Do your best to roll each piece of sticky dough into a smooth ball. It helps to fold the dough over itself, so that the top side of the ball has a tight smooth surface.

Make sure you place it seam side down on the parchment.

Preheat oven to 375 degrees.

Place the balls on two parchment lined baking sheets, four per sheet. Lightly cover and let rise for about 1.5 hours or until very puffy.

Lightly brush each bun with egg yolk (mix a yolk with a few drops of water). Sprinkle the tops with the extra crushed cornflakes.

Bake for about 15 to 18 minutes or until golden brown. Let cool on wire racks.

THE GOLDEN STATE KUMQUAT BURGER

I feel like this is sort of the ultimate California burger, reminding me of orange trees, and poppies in the bright sunlight. Of course, we will use poppy seed, not actual poppies, but I think the visualization still works. Avocado also makes a welcome addition to this burger.

Prep time:
15 minutes to cook and assemble,
25 minutes for the marmalade

Makes 4 burgers

To Make This Burger

- 1 pound ground beef
- 1 tablespoon Kumquat Marmalade (or store-bought orange marmalade)
- Leaf lettuce
- Thin shavings of manchego cheese
- Mayo
- Salt and pepper
- Cornflakes Poppy Seed Buns

Divide the beef into four equal patties, and generously salt and pepper. In pan or on grill, cook them for about 4 to 5 minutes, then flip for another 2 to 3 minutes.

Cut your buns and toast them.

Starting with the bottom bun, add a smear of mayo, the lettuce, then the burger patty, and the manchego cheese (don't melt it—in this case it's better if it's not melty). Then add a tablespoon of marmalade, and finally the top bun.

KUMQUAT MARMALADE

- 2 cups kumquats
- 1 Meyer lemon
- ½ cup sugar
- ½ cup water

Thinly slice the kumquats and the lemon, picking out the seeds as you go. The kumquat seeds are large, so it's pretty easy. Mix all in a heavy pot, and bring to a boil. Reduce to medium heat, and cook for about 20 minutes. Transfer to a Mason jar and refrigerate. (It'll set up as it cools). Will keep for a few weeks.

BLACK CHARCOAL SLIDER BUNS

These buns are crazy! Jet-black buns make a great photo at a Halloween party, but I think full sized black buns feel unappetizing. Instead, I like to make small slider buns, with a better filling to-bun ratio. You can find the activated charcoal online or in some health food stores. It's a superfine powder, so be careful, because you don't want this to get on the carpet!

Prep time:
30 minutes, plus about 2.5 hours to proof

Cook time:
15-18 minutes

Makes 16 buns

To Make This Bun

- 1 cup lukewarm water
- 2 tablespoons unsalted butter, cold, cut into pieces
- 1 large egg
- 3½ cups bread flour
- ¼ cup sugar
- 1¼ teaspoons salt
- 2 teaspoons active dry yeast
- 2 tablespoons activated charcoal
- 1 egg yolk (for egg wash)
- 2 tablespoons sesame seed and/or pretzel salt

In the mixer bowl, stir everything together except the egg yolk for the wash. Mix with the dough hook for about 5 minutes or until the dough forms one or more smooth balls.

If there are several balls, use your hands to combine. Cover with a towel for about 1 hour or until doubled in size.

Divide the dough into sixteen pieces. Do your best to roll each piece into a smooth ball. It helps to fold the dough over itself, so that the top side of the ball has a tight smooth surface. Make sure you place it seam side down on the parchment.

Preheat oven to 375 degrees.

Place the balls on two parchment lined baking sheets, eight per sheet. Lightly cover and let rise for about 1.5 hours or until very puffy.

Lightly brush each bun with egg yolk (mix a yolk with a few drops of water). Add the sesame seed or pretzel salt.

Bake for about 15 to 18 minutes or until golden brown. Let cool on wire racks.

COD CAKE SLIDERS

These are great little party burgers. Not only do they make a striking presentation with the jet-black buns and the colorful condiments, but they're really delicious, too! You can make the cod cakes and the related recipes ahead of time.

Prep time:
35 minutes to cook and assemble

Makes 4 burgers

To Make This Burger

- 4 Cod Cakes
- Pickled Red Onions
- Sweet Pickle Rémoulade
- Avocado slices
- Mango slices
- Salt and pepper
- Black Charcoal Slider Buns

Cook the Cod Cakes.

Cut your buns, and butter and toast them.

Starting with the bottom bun, add the rémoulade, then a cod cake, then the pickled onions with either mango slices or avocado (or go crazy and do both!), and finally add the top bun.

COD CAKES

- 6 ounces of cod or other firm white fish
- 1 large russet potato, peeled and cubed
- 1 clove garlic, peeled and chopped
- 1 tablespoons basil
- 2 tablespoons pine nuts
- 1 cup breadcrumbs
- Salt & pepper
- Oil for frying

Boil the cod in water for about 10 minutes until flaky. Boil the potatoes until soft. Let both cool a bit. Then lightly mash the potatoes and fish together, and mix in all the remaining ingredients. Let cool in the refrigerator for a few hours. Heat a pan with the olive oil. While the pan is heating, form the mash into golf ball sized balls, then flatten and fry in oil until golden brown on both sides.

PICKLED RED ONION

- 1 red onion, peeled and thinly sliced
- 3 tablespoons cider vinegar
- 2 tablespoons sugar
- 2 teaspoons fennel seed

Mix onion, sugar, cider vinegar, and fennel seed in a small bowl. Add just enough white vinegar to fully cover the onions. Let meld for a few hours, then keep refrigerated.

SWEET PICKLE RÉMOULADE

- ¼ cup Dijon mustard
- 1 cup mayo
- 2 teaspoons pickle juice
- 1 gherkin pickle, finely chopped
- 1 teaspoon hot sauce
- 1 garlic clove, chopped
- 1 tablespoon smoked paprika
- 2 teaspoons Cajun seasoning
- 1 tablespoon chopped parsley

Combine all ingredients, and refrigerate for a few hours to meld.

BLUE CHEESE POPPY SEED BUNS

These are soft, tangy buns, dotted with chunks of blue cheese. The trick is to fold the bits of cheese into the buns as you shape them. You want to keep the cheese inside, so it melts inside. When blue cheese melts on the outside, it's still yummy, but sometimes turns an odd pink color.

Prep time:
30 minutes, plus about 2.5 hours to proof

Cook time:
15-18 minutes

Makes 8 buns

To Make This Bun

- 1 cup lukewarm water
- 1 cup plain Greek yogurt
- 3¼ cups bread flour
- ¼ cup sugar
- 1¼ teaspoons salt
- 2 teaspoons active dry yeast
- 1 cup blue cheese chunks, in approximately half inch bits
- 1 egg yolk (for egg wash)
- Poppy seed

In the mixer bowl, stir everything together except the egg yolk for the wash, poppy seed, and blue cheese. Mix with the dough hook for about 5 minutes or until the dough forms one or more smooth balls.

If there are several balls, use your hands to combine. Cover with a towel for about 1 hour or until doubled in size.

Divide the dough into eight pieces. Flatten a piece of dough in your hand, place 3 or 4 good size chunks of cheese in the middle, and fold the dough up and around the cheese, trapping it fully inside. Roll the cheese-filled dough into a ball. It helps to fold the dough over itself, so that the top side of the ball has a tight smooth surface.

Preheat oven to 375 degrees.

Place the balls on two parchment lined baking sheets, four per sheet. Lightly cover and let rise for about 1.5 hours or until very puffy.

Lightly brush each bun with egg yolk (mix a yolk with a few drops of water). Sprinkle the tops with poppy seed or leave them off.

Bake for about 15 to 18 minutes or until golden brown. Let cool on wire racks.

AMERICAN
CHEDDAR
BRIE SWISS PEPPER JACK
MANCHEGO
CREAM CHEESE
GOAT GOUDA
BLUE

MUSHROOM SWISS BURGER

This is a classic combination: mushrooms, onions, Swiss, and blue cheese. I don't always like the shock of encountering a big chunk of blue cheese, but I do like the flavor. Here, the blue cheese is actually baked right into the buns, with little chunks of the melt oozing out, if you play your cards right. I added the Dill Pickle Rémoulade to give it a little sweet heat.

Prep time:
35 minutes to cook and assemble

Makes 4 burgers

To Make This Burger

- 1 pound ground beef
- Mushroom Sauté
- Dill Pickle Rémoulade
- Swiss cheese
- Red leaf lettuce
- Salt and pepper
- Blue Cheese Poppy Seed Buns

Divide the beef into four equal patties, and generously salt and pepper. In pan or on grill, cook them for about 4 to 5 minutes, then flip for another 2 to 3 minutes, and add a slice of Swiss cheese. When the cheese is melted, remove the burgers.

Cut your buns, and butter and toast them.

Starting with the bottom bun, add Dill Pickle Rémoulade, then a piece of lettuce, then the burger patty with melted cheese, a scoop of the mushroom sauté, and finally the top bun.

MUSHROOM SAUTÉ

- 1 tablespoon butter
- 1 cup thinly sliced onions
- 1 clove garlic, finely chopped
- 1 cup thinly sliced cremini mushrooms
- 1 tablespoon butter
- 1 tablespoon chopped fresh thyme or rosemary (or a mix of both)

On medium to low heat, sauté the onions and garlic in the butter for about 20 minutes, until they are soft and golden. Add the mushrooms, and cook another 5 minutes until soft. Add the herbs, and salt and pepper to taste.

DILL PICKLE RÉMOULADE

- ¼ cup Dijon mustard
- 1 cup mayo
- 2 teaspoon pickle juice
- 1 tablespoon finely chopped dill pickle
- 1 teaspoon hot sauce
- 1 garlic clove, chopped
- 1 tablespoon smoked paprika
- 2 teaspoons Cajun seasoning
- 1 tablespoon chopped parsley

Combine all ingredients, and refrigerate for a few hours to meld.

BRIOCHE BUTTERMILK BUNS

Soft, squishy buns like these are perfect for getting squashed in the Cubano Burger, but are also an all-around great bun. In fact, this bun could be used for any of the burgers in this book.

Prep time:
30 minutes, plus about 2.5 hours to proof

Cook time:
15-18 minutes

Makes 8 buns

To Make This Bun

- 1 cup slightly warm buttermilk
- 2 tablespoons unsalted butter, cold, cut into pieces
- 1 large egg
- 3½ cups bread flour
- ¼ cup sugar
- 1¼ teaspoons salt
- 2 teaspoons active dry yeast
- 1 egg yolk (for egg wash)
- 1 tablespoon Everything Bagel Seasoning

In the mixer bowl, stir everything together except the egg yolk for the wash. Mix with the dough hook for about 5 minutes or until the mix is a smooth ball.

Scoop the dough into a lightly oiled bowl. Move the dough ball around until it's oiled all over, then cover with a towel for about 1 hour or until its doubled in size.

Divide the dough into eight pieces. Do your best to roll each piece of sticky dough into a smooth ball. It helps to fold the dough over itself, so that the top side of the ball has a tight smooth surface.

Preheat oven to 375 degrees.

Place the balls on two parchment lined baking sheets, four per sheet. Lightly cover and let rise for about 1.5 hours or until very puffy.

Lightly brush each bun with egg yolk (mix a yolk with a few drops of water). Add any seeds, or leave them off.

Bake for about 15 to 18 minutes or until golden brown. Let cool on wire racks.

BREAD & BUTTER
DILL SOUR
SWEET
JALAPENO
GARLIC
CORNICHONS
KOSHER
GHERKIN
SWEET PEPPER

CUBANO BURGER

Cubanos, or Cuban sandwiches, have been around for a long time. They generally are roast pork, ham, Swiss cheese, pickles, and mustard, and then pressed between two pieces of bread and regrilled. I don't like a ton of extra meat on my burgers, so I left out the pork and just used ham. Be sure to thinly slice the pickles and try to cover the whole surface of the burger, so you can get a pickle in every bite!

Prep time:
35 minutes to cook and assemble

Makes 4 burgers

To Make This Burger

- 1 pound ground beef
- 4 slices of ham
- Swiss cheese
- Dill pickle spears
- Dijon mustard
- Salt and pepper
- Buttermilk Brioche Buns

Divide the beef into four equal patties, and generously salt and pepper. In pan or on grill, cook them for about 4 to 5 minutes, then flip for another 2 to 3 minutes, then flip again and add a slice of Swiss cheese. When the cheese is melted, remove the burgers, and place the ham in the hot pan or grill, and heat until it starts to brown.

Cut your buns, and butter and toast them.

Starting with the bottom bun, add the burger patty with melted cheese, the ham, the pickles, a squirt of mustard, and finally the top bun. Pick up the whole burger, and flip it into the hot pan, and gently push down to smash it a bit, until the top (now the bottom) gets a nice, crunchy sear. You can also squish it in a hot panini press, or just skip the regrilling part.

PEANUT BUTTER BUNS

We have a jar of powdered peanut butter that I bought for protein shakes, and it's been staring at me for weeks. Could I use it in a bun? Actual peanut butter resulted in a sticky disaster, but the powder? Perfect! The buns also have crushed peanuts inside and on top, for extra crunch.

Prep time:
30 minutes, plus about 1.5 hours to proof

Cook time:
15-18 minutes

Makes 8 buns

To Make This Bun

- 1 cup slightly warm buttermilk
- 2 tablespoons unsalted butter, cold, cut into pieces
- 1 large egg
- 3¼ cups bread flour
- ¼ cup sugar
- 1¼ teaspoons salt
- 2 teaspoons active dry yeast
- ½ cup powdered peanut butter
- ½ cup crushed peanuts
- 1 egg yolk (for egg wash)
- 2 tablespoons crushed peanuts for top

In the mixer bowl, stir everything together except the egg yolk for the wash and the peanuts reserved for the top). Mix with the dough hook for about 5 minutes or until the dough forms one or more smooth balls.

If there are several balls, use your hands to combine. Cover with a towel for about 1 hour or until doubled in size.

Divide the dough into four pieces. Do your best to roll each piece into a smooth ball. It helps to fold the dough over itself, so that the top side of the ball has a tight smooth surface. Make sure you place it seam side down on the parchment.

Preheat oven to 375 degrees.

Place the balls on two parchment lined baking sheets, four per sheet. Lightly cover, and let rise for about 1.5 hours or until very puffy.

Lightly brush each bun with egg yolk (mix a yolk with a few drops of water). Sprinkle the tops with crushed peanuts or leave them off.

Bake for about 15 to 18 minutes or until golden brown. Let cool on wire racks.

THE ELVIS BURGER

You'll get all shook up over this messy burger. It's a little of everything, salty, sweet, spicy, and satisfying. If you don't have fresh figs or fig jam, try grape jelly. Sounds cray, but it's a winning combination. Make sure you serve this with extra napkins!

Prep time:
15 minutes to cook and assemble

Makes 4 burgers

To Make This Burger

- 1 pound ground beef
- 8 strips of cooked bacon
- Fig jam or slice fresh figs
- Peanut butter
- Hot Honey
- Salt and pepper
- Peanut Butter Buttermilk Buns

Divide the beef into four equal patties, and generously salt and pepper. In pan or on grill, cook them for about 4 to 5 minutes, then flip for another 2 to 3 minutes.

Cut your buns, and butter and toast them.

Starting with the bottom bun, add peanut butter, then the burger patty, strips of bacon, some fig jam (or figs), and drizzle hot honey over everything. Finally, add the top bun.

HOT HONEY

- 1 cup honey
- 1 tablespoon chili flakes

Mix until fully combined.

SOFT PRETZEL BUNS

I once learned that you can essentially pretzel-ize any bread, not just pretzels. That discovery was the start of a quest, which resulted in this recipe. The buns aren't squishy-soft, but simply not as dense as a regular pretzel. It's a little tricky getting the unbaked buns in and out of the boiling solution, but you can do it! Note that you have only about 10 minutes to work, once it starts boiling, because it'll start to foam. A lot of foam. You'll see. Try to get it finished before the foam. Do you accept the challenge?

Prep time:
30 minutes, plus about 2 hours to proof

Cook time:
15-18 minutes

Makes 8 buns

To Make This Bun

- 1 cup lukewarm water
- 2 tablespoons unsalted butter, cold, cut into pieces
- 1 large egg
- 3½ cups bread flour
- ¼ cup sugar
- 1¼ teaspoons salt
- 2 teaspoons active dry yeast
- 2 gallons water
- 5 tablespoons baking soda
- 1 egg yolk (for egg wash)
- Pretzel salt
- Rice flour

In the mixer bowl, stir together the first seven ingredients. Mix with the dough hook for about 5 minutes or until the dough forms one or more smooth balls.

If there are several balls, use your hands to combine. Cover with a towel for about 1 hour or until doubled in size.

Divide the dough into eight pieces. Do your best to roll each piece into a smooth ball. It helps to fold the dough over itself, so that the top side of the ball has a tight smooth surface. Make sure you place it seam side down on the parchment.

Prepare a baking sheet with a piece of parchment, then lightly dust with rice flour. Do not skip this step! The rice flour will allow you to pick up the dough balls without them sticking to the parchment.

Place the balls onto the dusted parchment lined baking sheets, four per sheet. Lightly cover and let rise for about 1 hour or until puffy. Don't overproof or you won't be able to pick them up later.

Preheat oven to 375 degrees.

Bring to a boil in a large pot about 2 gallons of water and 5 tablespoons baking soda. Gently lift the dough balls from the parchment, and drop them into the boiling water a few at a time. Let them boil for about 40 seconds, then flip them and boil the other side for 40 more seconds. With a slotted spoon, lift them out and return them to the baking sheet, being careful to keep them facing the same way as when they were rising.

Lightly brush each bun with egg yolk (mix a yolk with a few drops of water). Sprinkle with pretzel salt. Using a razor blade, swiftly make a quarter inch deep slash across the tops. For a different look, you can slash an X.

Bake for about 15 to 18 minutes or until golden brown. Let cool on wire racks.

PRETZEL SALT

The big, white, non-melty salt you find on pretzels at the state fair is what you need to use. If you are taking the effort to make pretzel buns, regular salt just won't cut it. You can find it in specialty grocery stores, and on the web. It's called "pretzel salt."

HOMEMADE NACHO CHEESE BURGER

What's a worse snack for you than nacho cheese? This recipe probably still isn't great for you, but at least it's made from ingredients that you can pronounce and recognize. Making your own jalapeños also helps control what you are putting in your mouth.

Prep time:
25 minutes to cook and assemble

Makes 4 burgers

To Make This Burger

- 1 pound ground beef
- Nacho Cheese Sauce
- Quick Pickled Jalapeños
- Salt & pepper
- Pretzel Buns

Divide the beef into four equal patties, and generously salt and pepper. In pan or on grill, cook them for about 4 to 5 minutes, then flip for another 2 to 3 minutes.

Cut your buns, and butter and toast them.

Starting with the bottom bun, add the burger patty, spoon on the melted cheese, then pile on as many jalapeños as can fit. Finally, add the top bun.

NACHO CHEESE SAUCE

- 2 tablespoons butter
- 2 tablespoons flour
- 1 cup milk
- 1½ cup cheddar cheese, shredded
- ¼ teaspoon salt
- ¼ teaspoon smoked paprika

In a pot, whisk together the butter and flour and cook for about a minute, stirring constantly. On medium heat, add the milk and stir for a few minutes until the mixture starts to thicken. Turn off heat, add the cheese, salt and paprika, and slowly stir until the cheese is melted and a smooth.

QUICK PICKLED JALAPEÑOS

- ¾ cup water
- ¾ cup distilled white vinegar
- 3 tablespoons white sugar
- 1 tablespoon kosher salt
- 1 clove garlic, crushed
- 10 large jalapeño peppers, sliced into rings

In a big pot, bring everything to a boil except the peppers. Remove the pot from the heat, stir in the jalapeños, and let sit for about 15 minutes. Then pack the pepper rings into a clean Mason jar, adding enough vinegar mix to immerse them. Cover with a lid, and place in the refrigerator. They'll quickly turn olive green, and will be ready to eat the next day.

ROASTED RED PEPPER BUNS

Red peppers turn these buns a beautiful orange color. Make sure you use a seed topping, because they'll really look great in contrast to the bun color.

Prep time:
30 minutes, plus about 2.5 hours to proof

Cook time:
15-18 minutes

Makes 8 buns

To Make This Bun

- ½ cup lukewarm water
- ½ cup roasted red peppers (commercially prepared peppers are fine)
- 1 tablespoon smoked paprika
- 2 tablespoons unsalted butter, cold, cut into pieces
- 1 large egg
- 3 ¼ cups bread flour
- ¼ cup sugar
- 1 ¼ teaspoons salt
- 2 teaspoons active dry yeast
- 1 egg yolk (for egg wash)
- Sesame seed

In a blender, puree the roasted red peppers with the ½ cup of water. You'll need to use a cup of this puree. Gently heat the puree to lukewarm (warm to the touch, not hot).

In the mixer bowl, stir everything together except the egg yolk for the wash. Mix with the dough hook for about 5 minutes or until the dough forms one or more smooth balls.

If there are several balls, use your hands to combine. Cover with a towel for about 1 hour or until doubled in size.

Divide the dough into eight pieces. Do your best to roll each piece into a smooth ball. It helps to fold the dough over itself, so that the top side of the ball has a tight smooth surface. Make sure you place it seam side down on the parchment.

Preheat oven to 375 degrees.

Place the balls on two parchment lined baking sheets, four per sheet. Lightly cover and let rise for about 1.5 hours or until very puffy.

Lightly brush each bun with egg yolk (mix a yolk with a few drops of water). Sprinkle the tops with seeds, or leave them off.

Bake for about 15 to 18 minutes or until golden brown. Let cool on wire racks.

ROAST THE PEPPER!

You can used commercially prepared roasted peppers, but roasting your own is super easy. Cut out the stem, seeds, and white stuff, and slice into big wedges. Place the wedges on a foil-lined sheet (for speedy clean up), skin side up, and brush with olive oil. Put in hot oven (425 degrees, or under a broiler set on high) for about 15 minutes or until the skins are charred. Remove from oven, let cool, and then the skins will peel right off.

BLOODY MARY BURGER

Not sure if serving it with a Bloody Mary would be an overload, but this burger has all the flavors and fun of a Bloody Mary. Definitely a great brunch burger. Go crazy with your spear of condiments! A pickled shrimp, a hard-boiled egg, a mini-burger? It's your brunch, so be bold.

Prep time:
25 minutes to cook and assemble

Makes 4 burgers

To Make This Burger

- 1 pound ground beef
- Bloody Mary Mayo
- 8 strips cooked bacon
- Roasted red peppers
- Swiss cheese
- Leaf lettuce
- Pickles
- Celery salt
- Salt and pepper
- Roasted Red Pepper Buns
- Skewer of Bloody Mary additions: green olives, pickles, bacon, celery

Divide the beef into four equal patties, and generously salt and pepper. In pan or on grill, cook them for about 4 to 5 minutes, then flip for another 2 to 3 minutes, and add a slice of Swiss cheese. When the cheese is melted, remove the burgers.

Cut your buns, and butter and toast them.

Starting with the bottom bun, add Bloody Mary Mayo, a piece of lettuce, then the burger patty with melted cheese, then the bacon and roasted red peppers, a shake of celery salt, and finally the top bun. Spear the bun with a towering skewer of Bloody Mary goodies.

BLOODY MARY MAYO

- ½ cup mayo
- 1 teaspoon lemon juice
- 1 teaspoon hot sauce
- 1 teaspoon horseradish
- 1 teaspoon Worcestershire sauce

Mix until fully combined.

HONEY CORN BREAD BUNS

These buns will remind you of corn bread fresh from the oven. They won't rise quite as high as the all-flour buns, but the taste is incredible.

Prep time:
20 minutes, plus about 2.5 hours to proof

Cook time:
15-18 minutes

Makes 8 buns

To Make This Bun

- ½ cup warm milk
- ½ cup warm water
- 2 tablespoons honey
- 2 teaspoons active dry yeast
- 3 large egg yolks
- 2 teaspoons coarse salt
- 3 tablespoons unsalted butter, melted
- 1 cup yellow cornmeal
- 2 cups bread flour
- 1 egg yolk (for egg wash)

In the mixer bowl, stir together the warm milk, water, yeast, and sugar. Let stand until foamy, about 5 to 10 minutes. Add 3 egg yolks, salt, butter, cornmeal, and flour. Mix on low for about 7 to 10 minutes until the dough is nice and smooth, and just a little bit sticky.

Scoop the dough into a lightly oiled bowl. Move the dough ball around until it's oiled all over, then cover with a towel for about 1 hour or until its doubled in size.

Divide the dough into eight pieces. Do your best to roll each piece of sticky dough into a smooth ball. It helps to fold the dough over itself, so that the top side of the ball has a tight smooth surface.

Preheat oven to 400 degrees.

Place the balls on two parchment lined baking sheets, four per sheet. Lightly cover and let rise for about 30 more minutes.

Lightly brush each bun with egg yolk (mix a yolk with a few drops of water).

Bake for about 15 to 18 minutes or until golden brown. Let cool on wire racks.

PLANTAIN, FORBIDDEN RICE, AND SWEET POTATO BURGER

Tostones are a tasty little Latin American and Caribbean treat. Essentially they are double-fried plantains (those giant bananas at the store) and a little salt, they add a nice texture and sweetness to this veggie burger. I use black forbidden rice, but any rice will do. The black rice is striking to look at, and has almost a vanilla taste. Use it, if you can find it!

Prep time:
25 minutes to cook and assemble

Makes 4 burgers

To Make This Burger

- 4 Forbidden Rice Sweet Potato Burgers
- 8 tostones
- Honey Lime Slaw
- Lime Mayo
- Mayo
- Salt and pepper
- Honey Corn Bread Buns

Cut your buns, and butter and toast them.

Start with the bottom bun, add the lime mayo, a scoop of slaw, then the burger patty, two tostones, and finally add the top bun.

FORBIDDEN RICE SWEET POTATO BURGERS

- 2 cups cooked sweet potatoes
- 1 cup cooked black "forbidden rice" (or any cooked rice)
- ½ cup dry breadcrumbs
- 1 teaspoon smoked paprika
- 1 teaspoon garlic powder
- 1 teaspoon onion powder
- 1 teaspoon ground cumin
- 1 teaspoon salt
- 1 egg

In a bowl, using a fork, smash the sweet potatoes and rice into a paste. You don't need to mash them perfectly. Add all the other ingredients, and mix well.

Divide into patties, and cook in a bit of oil on medium heat for about 5 minutes per side or until they start turning golden brown.

TOSTONES

- 2 really dark plantains
- 2 tablespoons olive oil

Peel the plantains, and cut into one-inch chunks. Heat the oil in a large pan, and fry for about 3 minutes each side, until they start to brown.

Remove the chunks, and using a plate, smash them down to about a half inch high. Return to the pan, and fry on each side for about a minute. Salt to taste.

HONEY LIME SLAW

- Zest from one lime
- 3 tablespoons lime juice
- 2 tablespoons olive oil
- 1 tablespoon honey
- ½ teaspoon salt
- 2 cups shredded cabbage, carrots, or whatnot

Add everything except the cabbage to a small container with a tight-fitting lid, and shake it all up. Pour over the cabbage and toss. Keep chilled.

LIME MAYO

- Zest from one lime
- 3 tablespoons mayo

Mix it. Mix it well.

LEMON GREEN OLIVE BUNS

These are similar to the other green olive buns. But so what? I like green olives! I added lemon zest for a delightful flavor and scent.

Prep time:
30 minutes, plus about 2.5 hours to proof

Cook time:
15-18 minutes

Makes 8 buns

To Make This Bun

- 1 cup lukewarm water
- 2 tablespoons unsalted butter, cold, cut into pieces
- 1 large egg
- 3½ cups bread flour
- ¼ cup sugar
- 1¼ teaspoons salt
- 2 teaspoons active dry yeast
- 1 cup chopped green olives
- 2 tablespoons lemon zest
- 1 egg yolk (for egg wash)

In the mixer bowl, stir everything together except the egg yolk for the wash. Mix with the dough hook for about 5 minutes or until the dough forms one or more smooth balls.

If there are several balls, use your hands to combine. Cover with a towel for about 1 hour or until doubled in size.

Divide the dough into eight pieces. Do your best to roll each piece into a smooth ball. It helps to fold the dough over itself, so that the top side of the ball has a tight smooth surface. Make sure you place it seam side down on the parchment.

Preheat oven to 375 degrees.

Place the balls on two parchment lined baking sheets, four per sheet. Lightly cover, and let rise for about 1.5 hours or until very puffy.

Lightly brush each bun with egg yolk (mix a yolk with a few drops of water).

Bake for about 15-18 minutes or until golden brown. Let cool on wire racks.

CAULIFLOWER CAPER VEGGIE BURGER

Riced cauliflower is all the rage! It's easiest to buy it already grated. Grating at home can produce irregular results, with some pieces too big, and some ground to a puree. Don't omit the lemon slices in this recipe. Cut them as thin as you can, rind and all. Use only organic or homegrown lemons, because they haven't been sprayed with pesticides, and don't have a waxy coating.

Prep time:
25 minutes to cook and assemble

Makes 4 burgers

To Make This Burger

- 4 Cauliflower Caper Burgers
- Mayo
- Thinly sliced Meyer lemon
- Thinly sliced cucumber
- Leaf lettuce
- Salt and pepper
- Lemon Green Olive Buns

Cook your burgers as instructed below.

Cut your buns, and butter and toast them.

Starting with the bottom bun, add a smear of mayo, the lettuce, then the patty, then the sliced lemon and cucumber, and finally add the top bun.

CAULIFLOWER CAPER BURGERS

- 1 cup riced cauliflower, with as much water squeezed out as possible
- 1 cup cooked pinto beans
- 1 cup cooked quinoa
- ½ cup Panko breadcrumbs
- 1 tablespoon salt
- 2 eggs
- 2 tablespoons chopped parsley

Mix all the ingredients in a large bowl. Form into patties, then place them in refrigerator for at least an hour to firm up. In a hot pan, heat the olive oil, and cook the them until brown, about 3 minutes. Flip and brown the second side, about 3 more minutes.

POPPY SEED HONEY BUNS

This is another all-around good bun. What can go wrong with poppy seed inside and out?

Prep time:
30 minutes, plus about 2.5 hours to proof

Cook time:
15-18 minutes

Makes 8 buns

To Make This Bun

- 1 cup lukewarm water
- 2 tablespoons unsalted butter, cold, cut into pieces
- 1 large egg
- 3½ cups bread flour
- ¼ cup honey
- 1¼ teaspoons salt
- 2 teaspoons active dry yeast
- 2 tablespoons poppy seed
- 1 egg yolk (for egg wash)
- 2 tablespoons poppy seed for topping

In the mixer bowl, stir everything together except the egg yolk for the wash. Mix with the dough hook for about 5 minutes or until the dough forms one or more smooth balls.

If there are several balls, use your hands to combine. Cover with a towel for about 1 hour or until doubled in size.

Divide the dough into eight pieces. Do your best to roll each piece into a smooth ball. It helps to fold the dough over itself, so that the top side of the ball has a tight smooth surface. Make sure you place it seam side down on the parchment.

Preheat oven to 375 degrees.

Place the balls on two parchment lined baking sheets, four per sheet. Lightly cover and let rise for about 1.5 hours or until very puffy.

Lightly brush each bun with egg yolk (mix a yolk with a few drops of water). Top with more seeds.

Bake for about 15–18 minutes or until golden brown. Let cool on wire racks.

WHITE BEAN AND PEA SHOOT BURGER

This burger would be a great vegetarian option anytime of the year, but in the spring, pea shoots are specially available at our farmers markets. Fresh pea shoots taste like springtime. They are delightfully crunchy and taste mildly of peas. When I am lucky enough to get them, I put them on just about everything.

Prep time: 25 minutes to cook and assemble

Makes 4 burgers

To Make This Burger

- 4 White Bean Burgers
- Pea shoots
- Goat cheese
- Pickled red onions
- Avocado slices
- Mayo
- Salt and pepper
- Poppy Seed Honey Buns

Cut your buns, and butter and toast them.

Starting with the bottom bun, add the mayo, a layer of fresh pea shoots, then the burger patty, pickled red onions, and avocado. Crumble on some goat cheese, and finally add the top bun.

WHITE BEAN BURGERS

- 2 cups cooked white beans
- ½ cup dry breadcrumbs
- 1 teaspoon smoked paprika
- ½ teaspoon garlic powder
- ½ teaspoon onion powder
- ½ teaspoon ground cumin
- 1 teaspoon salt
- 1 egg

In a bowl, using a fork, smash the beans into a paste. You don't need to mash them perfectly. Add all the other ingredients, and mix well.

Divide into patties, and cook in a bit of oil on medium heat for about 5 minutes per side, or until they start turning golden brown.

PICKLED RED ONION

- 1 red onion, peeled and thinly sliced
- 3 tablespoons cider vinegar
- 2 tablespoons sugar
- 2 teaspoon fennel seedWhite vinegar

Mix onion, sugar, cider vinegar, and fennel seed in a small bowl. Add enough white vinegar to fully cover all the onions. Let meld for a few hours, then keep refrigerated.

RED BEET BUNS

Get ready for red hands and a red cutting board. It's a small price to pay for these red buns!

Prep time:
30 minutes, plus about 2.5 hours to proof

Cook time:
15-18 minutes

Makes 8 buns

To Make This Bun

- ½ cup lukewarm water
- ½ cup cooked beets
- 2 tablespoons unsalted butter, cold, cut into pieces
- 1 large egg
- 3¼ cups bread flour
- ¼ cup sugar
- 1¼ teaspoons salt
- 2 teaspoons active dry yeast
- 1 egg yolk (for egg wash)
- black sesame seed

In a blender, puree the beets with the ½ cup water. You'll need to use a cup of this puree. Gently heat the puree to lukewarm (warm to the touch, not hot).

In the mixer bowl, stir everything together except the egg yolk for the wash and the seeds. Mix with the dough hook for about 5 minutes, or until the dough forms one or more smooth balls.

If there are several balls, use your hands to combine. Cover with a towel for about 1 hour or until doubled in size.

Divide the dough into eight pieces. Do your best to roll each piece into a smooth ball. It helps to fold the dough over itself, so that the top side of the ball has a tight smooth surface. Make sure you place it seam side down on the parchment.

Preheat oven to 375 degrees.

Place the balls on two parchment lined baking sheets, four per sheet. Lightly cover and let rise for about 1.5 hours or until very puffy.

Lightly brush each bun with egg yolk (mix a yolk with a few drops of water). Sprinkle the tops with the seeds or leave them off.

Bake for about 15–18 minutes or until golden brown. Let cool on wire racks.

AUSSIE BURGER

I was working on the red beet bun when I came across something I had never heard of before: an "Aussie burger." I quickly texted my friend Toby, who is Australian, and asked, "Can this be true?" As it turns out it's very popular Down Under. I use fresh beets instead of pickling them, and, of course, a Red Beet Bun, but the rest is traditional.

Prep time:
25 minutes to cook and assemble

Makes 4 burgers

To Make This Burger

- 1 pound ground beef
- Sriracha Mayo
- Arugula
- 4 fresh pineapple rings
- 2 red beets, cooked and sliced
- 4 fried eggs
- salt and pepper
- Red Beet Buns

Divide the beef into four equal patties, and generously salt and pepper. In pan or on grill, cook them for about 4 to 5 minutes, then flip for another 2 to 3 minutes. Fry the eggs sunny-side up.

Cut your buns, and butter and toast them.

Starting with the bottom bun, add Sriracha Mayo, the arugula, a slice of pineapple, then the burger patty, the beets, the egg, and finally add the top bun.

SRIRACHA MAYO

- ½ cup mayo
- 2 tablespoons sriracha

Mix until fully combined.

POBLANO JACK BUNS

There's something about the combined flavor of roasted peppers and cheese that melts the heart. You can top these with *pepitas* like in the photo, or try topping with more chopped peppers and cheese, like with the Cheddar Jalapeños Buns.

Prep time:
20 minutes, plus about 2.5 hours to proof

Cook time:
25-30 minutes

Makes 8 buns

To Make This Bun

- ⅓ cup bread flour
- ¾ cup water
- 2½ cups bread flour
- 1 tablespoon white sugar
- 2 teaspoons yeast
- 1 teaspoon sea salt
- ½ cup roasted poblano pepper, skinned and finely chopped
- ¾ cup diced Monterey Jack cheese
- 1 egg
- ½ cup milk
- ¼ cup softened butter
- 1 egg yolk (for egg wash)
- 2 tablespoons pepitas

In a small saucepan over medium heat, whisk the smaller amount of bread flour and the water (the first two ingredients listed) until it becomes a smooth, thick paste. Let cool for a bit.

Get out your electric mixer with a dough hook. Mix the next four dry ingredients together in the bowl. In a separate bowl, whisk the egg and milk together. With the mixer on low speed, slowly add the egg/milk mixture. Then add the flour paste you made earlier.

Mix on medium speed for another 5 minutes. Then break the softened butter into lumps, and toss them into the mixer as it's going. Mix for 3 minutes more. The dough will look smooth, but will be super sticky.

Scoop the dough into a lightly oiled bowl. Move the dough ball around until it's oiled all over, then cover with a towel for about 1 hour or until doubled in size.

When the dough is big and puffy, it's time to form the buns. Dump the dough onto a cutting board. It'll deflate, but don't worry, the yeast is still working for you. Divide the dough into eight pieces. Do your best to roll each piece of sticky dough into a smooth ball. It helps to fold the dough over itself, so that the top side of the ball has a tight smooth surface.

Preheat oven to 325 degrees.

Place the balls on two parchment lined baking sheets, four per sheet. (This is just for looks. I like a bun that hasn't baked in contact with another bun. You can space them all out on one sheet, but they may rise into each other.) Let rise for about 20 minutes.

Lightly brush each bun with egg yolk (mix a yolk with a few drops of water), then generously sprinkle with pepitas.

Bake at 325 degrees for 25–30 minutes or until the tops start to brown. Let cool on wire racks.

ELOTE BURGER

When I was a kid growing up in the Ohio suburbs, you could drive about ten minutes and be in a corn field. There was a little hut, where the Corn Man would be all summer, selling freshly picked corn. My mom would come home with a few grocery bags full, and make my brothers and me shuck them. I remember eating the ears boiled in water, and then slathered in butter and salt and pepper. Fast-forward forty years. By now I've been introduced to many other ways to prepare fresh corn, such as *elote*, but I'm not sure I've ever had corn as good as what the Corn Man sold. This elote salad makes it possible to get the elote onto a burger.

Prep time:
25 minutes to cook and assemble

Makes 4 burgers

To Make This Burger

- 8 Cheddar Corn Cakes
- Elote Salad
- Radishes
- Arugula
- Cotija cheese
- Tajin spice, or Cajun seasoning
- Salt and pepper
- Poblano and Jack Buns

Cook the burgers. Cut your buns, and butter and toast them.

Starting with the bottom bun, add a handful of arugula, then stack two corn cakes, and spoon on the Elote Salad. Add a few fresh radish slices, shake on a spoonful of dry Cotija and Tajin spice, and finally add the top bun.

CHEDDAR CORN CAKES

- 2 cups fresh or thawed frozen corn
- 1 medium onion, diced
- 1 clove garlic, chopped
- 2 tablespoons unsalted butter

- 1½ teaspoons baking powder
- ½ teaspoon salt
- ½ teaspoon black pepper
- 2 eggs
- ½ cup milk
- ½ cup shredded cheddar cheese
- 1 cup flour

In a large pan, melt the butter, and gently sauté the onions and garlic until soft. Then add the corn, and cook for about 5 minutes.

In a large bowl, mix together all the other ingredients. Thoroughly stir in the cooked corn mixture.

Cook the corn cakes just like pancakes. Heat a little butter or oil in a pan. Pour about ⅓ cup of the mixture into the pan. If the pan is big enough, make several at the same time. Cook for about 3 minutes, then flip and cook for about 3 more, or until golden brown on both sides.

ELOTE SALAD

- 1 cup fresh or thawed frozen corn
- ¼ cup mayo
- 1 tablespoon fresh lime juice
- ½ teaspoon salt
- ½ teaspoon black pepper
- 2 teaspoons finely chopped jalapeños (seeds removed before chopping)
- 2 teaspoons Tajin spice
- ¼ cup Cotija cheese

Mix all the ingredients.

DUTCH CRUNCH BUNS

Dutch crunch bread was always my choice for sandwiches, but I had never seen its topping used on a bun. Turns out, it's not difficult to turn a regular bun into a crunchy, crackly-topped wonder.

Prep time:
30 minutes, plus about 1.5 hours to proof

Cook time:
15-18 minutes

Makes 8 buns

To Make This Bun

- 1 cup lukewarm water
- 2 tablespoons unsalted butter, cold, cut into pieces
- 1 large egg
- 3½ cups bread flour
- ¼ cup sugar
- 1¼ teaspoons salt
- 2 teaspoons active dry yeast

Crunch Topping

- 2 teaspoons active dry yeast
- ¾ cup lukewarm water
- 1 tablespoon sugar
- 1 tablespoon olive oil
- ¼ teaspoon salt
- 1 cup rice flour

In the mixer bowl, stir everything together. Mix with the dough hook for about 5 minutes, or until the dough forms one or more smooth balls.

If there are several balls, use your hands to combine. Cover with a towel for about 1 hour or until doubled in size.

Divide the dough into eight pieces. Do your best to roll each piece into a smooth ball. It helps to fold the dough over itself, so that the top side of the ball has a tight smooth surface. Make sure you place it seam side down on the parchment.

Preheat oven to 375 degrees.

Place the balls on two parchment lined baking sheets, four per sheet. Lightly cover and let rise for about 1.5 hours or until very puffy.

For the crunch topping, mix together all the crunch ingredients, and let rest for about 15 minutes until it puffs up a bit.

With a dinner knife, spread a layer of the mix over the tops and sides of each bun, as if you were frosting a cupcake. Use a gentle hand, so you don't deflate the buns.

Let sit for about 20 more minutes.

Bake for about 15–18 minutes, or until golden brown. Let cool on wire racks.

SOUTHWEST BEAN AND CORN BURGER

I'm not sure there's anything Southwestern about Dutch crunch buns, but this is a veggie burger that works! Crunchy buns, a little heat, and a ton of flavor make this a hearty burger for all. The Poblano Jack Bun or the Cheddar Jalapeño Bun would be perfect here, too.

Prep time:
25 minutes to cook and assemble

Makes 4 burgers

To Make This Burger

- 4 Black Bean Corn Burgers
- Chipotle Salsa
- Pepper jack cheese
- Mayo
- Leaf lettuce
- Avocado
- Salt and pepper
- Dutch Crunch Buns

Cook the burgers, and melt a slice of Pepper Jack on each.

Cut your buns, and butter and toast them.

Starting with the bottom bun, add the mayo, the lettuce, then the burger patty, some avocado slices, then spoon on the salsa, and finally add the top bun.

BLACK BEAN CORN BURGERS

- 1 can black beans, drained and rinsed
- ½ cup cooked *farro*
- 1 cup corn
- 1 teaspoon garlic powder
- 1 teaspoon chili powder
- 1 egg
- ½ cup seasoned breadcrumbs
- Salt and pepper to taste

In a bowl, using a fork, smash the beans into a paste. You don't need to mash them perfectly. Add all the other ingredients.

Divide into patties, and cook in a bit of oil on medium heat for about 5 minutes per side, or until they start turning golden brown.

CHIPOTLE SALSA

- 2 28-ounce cans fire roasted tomatoes
- ½ cup fresh cilantro
- ½ cup chopped onion
- 1 clove garlic, minced
- 1 whole jalapeño, with seeds removed
- 1 teaspoon ground cumin
- 1 teaspoon salt
- 1 teaspoon sugar
- 2 tablespoons canned chipotles, chopped
- Juice of one lime

Put all ingredients in a large blender or food processor, and pulse until still a little chunky. Put in Mason jars, and refrigerate.

POPCORN BUNS

Corny and a tad spicy, these buns topped with popcorn will make your head pop. Make sure not to overbake, or the popcorn will start to burn. Also, make sure you crush the popcorn, or it won't stick well.

Prep time:
30 minutes, plus about 1.5 hours to proof

Cook time:
15-18 minutes

Makes 8 buns

To Make This Bun

- 1 cup lukewarm water
- 2 tablespoons unsalted butter, cold, cut into pieces
- 1 large egg
- 2 cups bread flour
- 1½ cups fine ground cornmeal
- ¼ cup sugar
- 1¼ teaspoons salt
- 2 teaspoons active dry yeast
- 1 tablespoon crushed red pepper
- 1 egg yolk (for egg wash)
- Crushed popcorn

In the mixer bowl, stir together everything except the egg yolk for the wash. Mix with the dough hook for about 5 minutes, or until the dough forms one or more smooth balls.

If there are several balls, use your hands to combine. Cover with a towel for about 1 hour or until doubled in size.

Divide the dough into eight pieces. Do your best to roll each piece into a smooth ball. It helps to fold the dough over itself, so that the top side of the ball has a tight smooth surface. Make sure you place it seam side down on the parchment.

Preheat oven to 375 degrees.

Place the balls on two parchment lined baking sheets, four per sheet. Lightly cover and let rise for about 1.5 hours or until very puffy.

Lightly brush each bun with egg yolk (mix a yolk with a few drops of water). Sprinkle crushed popcorn on top.

Bake for about 15–18 minutes, or until golden brown. Let cool on wire racks.

FIGS AND HONEY BURGER

This is like a cheese plate turned into a burger. Figs, manchego cheese—some sweetness plus a little spiciness. The corn bread and popcorn flavors in the bun work really well with this burger.

Prep time:
15 minutes to cook and assemble

Makes 4 burgers

To Make This Burger

- 1 pound ground beef
- Fig jam or sliced fresh figs
- Hot Honey
- Manchego cheese
- Arugula
- Mayo
- Salt and pepper
- Popcorn Buns

Divide the beef into four equal patties, and generously salt and pepper. In pan or on grill, cook them for about 4 to 5 minutes, then flip for another 2 to 3 minutes.

Cut your buns, and butter and toast them.

Starting with the bottom bun, and add mayo, then arugula, the burger patty, and a few slices of manchego cheese. Top that with fig jam (or figs), drizzle Hot Honey over everything, and finally add the top bun.

HOT HONEY

- 1 cup honey
- 1 tablespoon chili flakes

Mix until fully combined.

LEMON POPPY SEED BUNS

Like a lemon poppy seed muffin, but a bun. It'll catch you off guard, because something in your brain will be expecting this to taste sweet, but removing the sweetness makes the lemon and poppy seed flavors shine.

Prep time:
30 minutes, plus about 2.5 hours to proof

Cook time:
15-18 minutes

Makes 8 buns

To Make This Bun

- 1 cup lukewarm water
- 2 tablespoons unsalted butter, cold, cut into pieces
- 1 large egg
- 2 cups bread flour
- 1½ cups fine ground cornmeal
- ¼ cup sugar
- 1¼ teaspoons salt
- 2 teaspoons active dry yeast
- 2 tablespoons poppy seedzest from one large lemon
- 1 egg yolk (for egg wash)

In the mixer bowl, stir together everything except the egg yolk for the wash. Mix with the dough hook for about 5 minutes, or until the dough forms one or more smooth balls.

If there are several balls, use your hands to combine. Cover with a towel for about 1 hour or until doubled in size.

Divide the dough into eight pieces. Do your best to roll each piece into a smooth ball. It helps to fold the dough over itself, so that the top side of the ball has a tight smooth surface. Make sure you place it seam side down on the parchment.

Preheat oven to 375 degrees.

Place the balls on two parchment lined baking sheets, four per sheet. Lightly cover and let rise for about 1.5 hours or until very puffy.

Lightly brush each bun with egg yolk (mix a yolk with a few drops of water).

Bake for about 15–18 minutes or until golden brown. Let cool on wire racks.

BLUEBERRY SALMON BURGER

While living the Pacific Northwest, I fell in love with the flavor combination of blueberries and salmon. Bears eat both berries and fish, so I'll bet they'd love this burger. It can be a sweet burger, depending on how much sauce you use. If cream cheese isn't your jam, brie would be another great choice.

Prep time:
15 minutes to make the sauce and assemble

Makes 4 burgers

To Make This Burger

- 4 Salmon Burgers
- Blueberry Sauce
- Cream cheese
- Leaf lettuce
- Salt and pepper
- Lemon Poppy Seed Buns

Cut your buns, and butter and toast them.

Starting with the bottom bun, add the mayo, the lettuce, then the salmon patty, and spoon on the blueberries. Finally, add the top bun.

SALMON BURGERS

- 2 cups flaked cooked salmon
- ½ cup dry breadcrumbs
- 1 egg
- 1 teaspoon smoked paprika
- 1 teaspoon salt
- 1 tablespoon chopped chives

In a bowl, using a fork, mix all the ingredients. It's OK to keep some of the larger salmon chunks.

Divide into patties, and cook in a bit of oil on medium heat for about 5 minutes per side or until they start turning golden brown.

BLUEBERRY SAUCE

- 1 cup fresh or frozen blueberries

Heat berries gently in a pan until they start to pop and get juicy. That's it. Is this even a recipe?

VEGAN WHOLE WHEAT BUNS

These vegan whole wheat buns are pillowy soft and delicious. These are the only buns in the book that don't get brushed or topped with anything at the end. If you must have seeds, you can brush the buns with a little oil, and sprinkle on the seeds, but most will fall off when you pick up the cooked bun. But the whole wheat gives these guys a beautiful color, so it's best to leave them in the buff.

Prep time:
30 minutes, plus about 2.5 hours to proof

Cook time:
15-18 minutes

Makes 8 buns

To Make This Bun

- 1 cup lukewarm water
- ⅓ cup olive oil
- 2 cups bread flour
- 1½ cups whole wheat flour
- ¼ cup sugar
- 1¼ teaspoons salt
- 2 teaspoons active dry yeast

In the mixer bowl, stir together. Mix with the dough hook for about 5 minutes, or until the dough forms one or more smooth balls.

If there are several balls, use your hands to combine. Cover with a towel for about 1 hour or until doubled in size.

Divide the dough into eight pieces. Do your best to roll each piece into a smooth ball. It helps to fold the dough over itself, so that the top side of the ball has a tight smooth surface. Make sure you place it seam side down on the parchment.

Place the balls on two parchment lined baking sheets, four per sheet. Lightly cover and let rise for about 1.5 hours or until very puffy.

Preheat oven to 375 degrees.

Bake for about 15–18 minutes or until golden brown. Let cool on wire racks.

VEGAN QUINOA BURGER WITH CURRY SAUCE

This burger is all vegan, and according to my wife, Lori, it's one of the best in the book! It's hearty and protein-packed. The mango salsa adds a punch of heat and a kick of sweetness. And the sauce. Let's talk about the sauce. It's a knockoff from a poplar veggie restaurant in Oregon, an odd mix of flavors and ingredients, but it comes together as a tangy, curry-spiked flavor-bomb. The sauce recipe makes enough to fill a quart Mason jar, which is great, because you'll also want to use the sauce on rice and bean bowls, and on salads.

Prep time:
15 minutes to make the sauce and assemble

Makes 4 burgers

To Make This Burger

- 4 Quinoa Burgers
- Curry Sauce
- Mango Salsa
- Leaf lettuce
- Salt and pepper
- Vegan Whole Wheat Buns

Cut your buns, and oil and toast them.

QUINOA BURGERS

- ½ cup cooked quinoa
- 1 cup cooked black beans
- ½ cup caramelized onions
- ½ cup raw walnuts
- ½ cup rolled oats
- 1 teaspoon Dijon mustard
- 1 teaspoon garlic powder
- 1 teaspoon onion powder
- 1 teaspoon salt

In a blender or food processor, grind the walnuts and oats together, leaving some coarse pieces.

In a bowl, using a fork, mix all the ingredients. Refrigerate for a few hours, so the nuts and oats can soften.

Divide into patties, and cook in a bit of oil on medium heat for about 5 minutes per side or until they start turning golden brown.

CURRY SAUCE

- ½ cup avocado oil
- ½ cup slivered almonds
- 1 can garbanzo beans, including the liquid
- ½ cup coconut milk
- ½ cup fresh lemon juice
- 2 garlic cloves, minced
- ½ teaspoon coarse kosher salt
- 1 teaspoon curry powder
- 1 teaspoon garlic powder
- 1⅓ cup nutritional yeast

Blend until smooth. Refrigerate. This will get better after a day or two.

MANGO SALSA

- 1 large ripe mango (about a cup of chopped fruit)
- ¼ cup diced red onion
- ¼ cup chopped cilantro
- 1 small jalapeño, seeds removed and diced
- 1 garlic clove, minced
- ½ teaspoon salt
- Juice from one lime

Mix all ingredients. Let sit for about an hour to meld flavors.

LEEK, CHEDDAR, AND BACON WAFFLES

I recently bought a little waffle maker. I love it. It makes only one four-inch waffle at a time, so it takes forever, but you get perfect burger-sized waffles! I'm pretty sure you can add anything to the waffle recipe, and it will be delicious.

Prep time:
30 minutes

Cook time:
15-18 minutes

Makes 8 mini waffles

To Make This Waffle

- 1 cup bread flour
- ½ teaspoon salt
- 2 teaspoons baking powder
- 1 cup milk
- 1 large egg
- 2 tablespoons melted butter
- ½ cup shredded cheddar cheese
- ½ cup chopped, cooked bacon
- 1 tablespoons olive oil
- ½ cup caramelized leeks

In a bowl, stir together the dry ingredients, then add the milk, egg, and butter, stirring until just mixed. Gently fold in the bacon, cheese, and leeks. Let the batter rest for about 15 minutes.

Heat a waffle iron, grease with oil or butter, then cook waffles in batches until golden brown.

CARAMELIZED LEEKS

- 2 cups thinly sliced leeks, the white part and just a bit of the green
- 1 tablespoon olive oil
- 1 teaspoon salt

In a pan on low heat, heat a tablespoon olive oil, and gently cook the sliced leeks for about a half hour, stirring every few minutes to keep from burning.

PIMENTO CHEDDAR BACON WAFFLE BURGER

This is a delicious little bacony, cheesy stack of goodness. The pimento cheese adds some spicy creaminess, and the arugula adds a touch of bitterness. You'll never want regular waffles again.

Prep time:
25 minutes to make the waffles and assemble

Makes 4 burgers

To Make This Burger

- 1 pound ground beef
- 8 strips cooked bacon
- Cheddar Crisps
- Pimento Cheese
- Arugula
- Mayo
- Salt and pepper
- Leek, Cheddar, and Bacon Waffles

Divide the beef into four equal patties, and generously salt and pepper. In pan or on grill, cook them for about 4 to 5 minutes, then flip for another 2 to 3 minutes.

Starting with the bottom waffle, add mayo, the arugula, and then the burger patty with a smear of pimento cheese. Top with bacon and Cheddar Crisps, and finally add the top waffle.

PIMENTO CHEESE

- 1 cup shredded cheddar cheese
- 4 ounce jar of pimentos, drained
- 4 tablespoons cream cheese, softened
- ½ cup mayonnaise
- ¼ teaspoon garlic powder
- ¼ teaspoon smoked paprika
- ¼ teaspoon cayenne pepper

Mix and refrigerate for about an hour to blend flavors.

CHEDDAR CRISPS

- 1 cup shredded cheddar cheese

Sprinkle ¼ cup of cheese in the middle of a hot pan, and let it melt. After about a minute, the cheese will start to crisp and brown. Flip and crisp the other side. Repeat with the remaining cheese.

GREEN ONION BLACK PEPPER WAFFLES

I love green onions. I love black pepper. I love these waffles.

Prep time:
30 minutes

Cook time:
15-18 minutes

Makes 8 mini waffles

To Make This Waffle

- 1 cup bread flour
- ½ teaspoon salt
- 2 teaspoons baking powder
- 1 cup milk
- 1 large egg
- 2 tablespoons melted butter
- ½ cup chopped green onions
- 1 tablespoon black pepper

In a bowl, stir together the dry ingredients, then add the milk, egg and butter, stirring until just mixed. Gently fold in the green onions and pepper. Let the batter rest for about 15 minutes.

Heat a waffle iron, grease with oil or butter, then cook waffles in batches until golden brown.

BLACK GARLIC AND ASPARAGUS WAFFLE BURGER

Black garlic is something from another world. It's just regular garlic that has been heated super slowly and cooked for weeks. You can find it in high-end grocery stores, Asian markets, or online. A little goes a *long* way, so go lightly at first. It's a little bit sweet, a little bit funky, but it makes this crazy burger awesome.

Prep time:
25 minutes to make the waffles and assemble

Makes 4 burgers

To Make This Burger

- 1 pound ground beef
- Steamed asparagus
- Black Garlic Mayo
- Cream cheese
- Salt and pepper
- Green Onion Pepper Waffles

Divide the beef into four equal patties, and generously salt and pepper. In pan or on grill, cook them for about 4 to 5 minutes, then flip for another 2 to 3 minutes.

Starting with the bottom waffle, add black garlic mayo, then the burger patty with a smear of cream cheese, then asparagus spears, and finally add the top waffle.

BLACK GARLIC MAYO

- 1 cup mayo
- 1–2 cloves of black garlic

Smash the cloves on a cutting board, and smear them out into a paste. Add to the mayo, and mix. Refrigerate for about an hour to blend flavors.

GREEN ONION PITA BREAD

Pita is a pretty easy bread to master, but it does require some patience. Any extra pitas can be turned into pita pizzas or chopped up and toasted, to make fun salad croutons.

Prep time:
15 minutes plus about 2 hours to proof

Cook time:
3-5 minutes each

Makes 8 pitas

To Make This Pita

- 1 cup warm water
- 2 teaspoons active dry or instant yeast
- 3 cups bread flour
- 2 tablespoons finely chopped green onion
- 1 tablespoon poppy seed2 teaspoons salt

In the mixer bowl, stir together all the ingredients. Then mix on low for about 5 to 7 minutes.

Scoop the dough into a lightly oiled bowl. Move the dough ball around until it's oiled all over, then cover with a towel for about 1 to 2 hours or until doubled in size.

Put your baking stone into the oven, if you have one. If not, put in a baking sheet. Preheat oven to 450 degrees.

Divide the dough into eight pieces and roll into balls. On a floured surface, flatten the balls with a rolling pin, until they are about eight inches across. If they shrink, let them rest for a few minutes, then roll some more. They will eventually behave.

Until you get the hang of it, toss only one dough disk at a time onto the hot stone or baking sheet. After about a minute it should start to puff up like a whoopee cushion. When fully puffed, pull it out with tongs, and cook another.

Remember, a watched pita never puffs.

GREEK PITA BURGER

Most of the time, when you hear "Greek burger," it's going to be gross, because it will be made from lamb. Just kidding—each to their own. I personally do not like lamb, so my Greek Pita Burger is beef, and has beets, which is weird but delicious, and uses a pita that you'll never find in stores. Give it a try!

Prep time:
15 minutes to make the waffles and assemble

Makes 4 burgers

To Make This Burger

- 1 pound ground beef
- Tzatziki
- Roasted yellow beets, sliced
- Leaf lettuce
- Gherkin or dill pickles
- Salt & pepper
- Green Onion Pita Bread

Divide the beef into four equal patties, and generously salt and pepper. In pan or on grill, cook them for about 4 to 5 minutes, then flip for another 2 to 3 minutes.

Cut the top inch or so off the round pita, and pry it open.

To assemble, first put in a layer of lettuce, then a few beet rounds and thinly sliced pickles, then slide the in the burger patty, and spoon the sauce over all the fillings. Serve with a little more sauce on the side.

TZATZIKI

- 1 small container Greek yogurt (Plain! Not vanilla! Sorry for yelling, but admit it, you were reaching for vanilla.)
- Half a cucumber, peeled, deseeded, and chopped
- 1 clove garlic, finely chopped
- Juice from half a lemon
- 2 tablespoons fresh herbs, such as dill, basil, cilantro, parsley, or thyme
- 1 teaspoon salt

Combine ingredients, and refrigerate until ready to use.

ENGLISH MUFFINS

English muffins will take longer than your normal buns, but with a little planning, you can do this! The reward of homemade English muffins is well worth it. This recipe will make a good size batch. You can freeze the extra, and use as needed for your butter and jelly delivery needs.

Prep time:
Prep time: 30 minutes plus about 6 hours to proof (PLUS, you need to start the leaven the night before! Don't forget!)

Cook time:
15-18 minutes each

Makes 20 four-inch English muffins

To Make This English Muffin

Leaven

- 1¾ cups water
- 1¾ bread flour

Dough

- 2 teaspoons active dry yeast
- 2 cups warm water
- 3½ cups bread flour
- 1 tablespoon salt
- Rice flour for dusting
- Clarified butter

Mix the Leaven

The night before you bake, measure out the water, flour, and yeast into a Tupperware bowl, and mix. Place a towel over the bowl, and let sit until morning, when it should be nice and bubbly.

Mix Dough

In a large bowl, add the 2 cups warm water (warm but not hot). With a wet hand, scoop the bubbly leaven into the water, and squish it around until all the big globs

are gone. Add the 3½ cups bread flour and the salt, and thoroughly mix with your hands. Cover bowl, and let rest. After 30 minutes, gently turn the dough, and pull and stretch it a few times. Repeat this stretch and pull every 30 minutes for about 2.5 hours. After about 3 hours, the dough will have noticeably risen, and will have a smooth look. Dump the dough onto a cutting board heavily dusted with rice flour. With a cutter, divide the dough into two equal pieces.

Take two baking sheets, lay flat a dish towel on each, and heavily dust with rice flour.

Gently pull and stretch one of the pieces into a rectangle, and place on one of the baking sheets. Try to make the piece uniformly about an inch thick. Don't worry about the shape. Repeat with the second piece of dough and the other baking sheet. Cover and let sit for 3 hours, or put them in the fridge until the next day.

Making English Muffins

Uncover a tray of dough, and sprinkle on more rice flour. Lay a cutting board on top, and flip it over, transferring the dough to the cutting board. Use a three- or four-inch English muffin ring to cut out the muffins, by gently pushing down and twisting.

On an electric griddle, brush the hot surface with clarified butter. Over medium to high heat, cook the muffins for about 4 to 5 minutes per side, brushing the tops before flipping. Muffins are done when they turn golden brown.

ENGLISH MUFFIN "BREAKFAST FOR DINNER" BURGER

Who doesn't like breakfast for dinner? This burger mimics a McDonald's Egg McMuffin, but takes it up a notch, turning it into a burger. Make sure you press down the potatoes while cooking, so they stick together to make a nice potato nest. Cooking the egg just right will also give you that nice drippy yolk. This could also be a "Dinner for Breakfast" Burger, depending on when you eat it.

Prep time:
25 minutes to cook and assemble

Makes 4 burgers

To Make This Burger

- 1 pound ground beef
- 4 hash brown patties
- 4 slices cooked bacon
- American cheese
- 4 eggs
- Mayo
- Leaf lettuce
- Salt and pepper
- English Muffins

Divide the beef into four equal patties, and generously salt and pepper. In a hot pan, smash down the patty and let it cook for a minute. Flip it, and top with a slice of American cheese. Cook the burger about 4 to 5 more minutes, until cheese is melted.

Cook the egg sunny-side up: In same pan, add a little more oil or butter, then gently crack the eggs in the pan, doing your best to keep them separate. (You can also cook the eggs in batches.) Cook them until all the clear parts have turned white. You can speed this up by temporarily placing a lid on the pan. Just don't over-cook, or you won't get that runny yolk yumminess. Salt and pepper.

Toast the English Muffins in the toaster.

Starting with the bottom muffin, spread a little mayo, and add the lettuce, and the burger with melted cheese. Then add a Hash Brown Patty, the bacon, and the sunny-side up egg. Finally, add the top muffin.

HASH BROWN PATTIES

- 2 cups shredded potatoes
- 1 tablespoon oil
- Salt & pepper

Drop the shredded potatoes into cold water, and flush around until the water is cloudy. Rinse, then do it again. Heat a pan, add a little oil or butter, and then the potatoes. Spread them out, and cook on medium for about 6 minutes. Then flip and cook the other side for about 6 more minutes or until nicely browned and crisp. On that second flip, try to smash them together so they become a mat of potato. Salt and pepper generously. Remove and divide into four portions.

Or save time by buying pre-shredded frozen hash browns!

CIABATTA BUNS

This recipe is a little trickier than the regular buns, mainly because the dough will be wetter. So make sure to use plenty of extra flour for dusting the surfaces, so it doesn't stick.

Prep time: over-night rise for starter, plus about 3 hours for dough

Bake time: 22 minutes

Makes 8 buns

To Make This Bun

Starter

- 1 ¼ cup bread flour
- 1 teaspoon active dry yeast
- 1 teaspoon sugar
- 1 cup water

Dough

- 2 ¼ cups bread flour
- 1 teaspoon sugar
- 1 teaspoon salt
- 2 teaspoons active dry yeast
- ½ cup warm milk
- 2 tablespoons olive oil

Make the Starter

The night before, in a small bowl, mix the starter ingredients into a paste. Cover with a towel, and leave on the counter. In the morning, it'll be puffy and ready to go!

Make the Bread

In a large bowl, add the milk, then add the puffy starter. Using your fingers, break apart the starter as best you can. Add 2 cups of the flour, and the salt, yeast, sugar and oil. Stir with your hand (it works best!), or with a big spoon, until it all comes together. It'll be very sticky.

Sprinkle the final ¼ cup of flour on a board, and scrape the dough onto the floured surface. Knead the dough for about 5 minutes, until it gets smoother and stops sticking. Form it into a ball, and move it to a bowl, oiled, so it won't stick. Cover, and let rise for 2 hours.

Move the dough back to a lightly floured board. Using a dough scraper, divide it into eight equal pieces. Take a parchment lined baking sheet, and generously dust with more flour. Take one piece of dough, and gently fold it like a sheet of paper folded to fit an envelope, with one third folded in, and the last third folded over the first. It'll look somewhat like a little burrito. Now tuck the ends under, so no seams show. Repeat for the remaining pieces, and space them out evenly on the floured sheets.

Cover and let rise for 2 more hours.

Bake at 425 degrees for 22 minutes or until golden brown.

BÁNH MÌ BURGER

Bánh mì are my all-time favorite sandwiches. I've taken the ingredients, and turned it into a zippy burger. Traditionally, you would use a French baguette, but I'm replacing that with a more bun-like Ciabatta roll. This burger definitely brings both the sweet and the heat.

Prep time:
15 minutes to cook and assemble

Makes 4 burgers

To Make This Burger

- 1 pound ground beef
- Quick Pickled Veggies
- Cilantro
- 1 jalapeño, thinly sliced
- Sriracha Mayo
- Salt & pepper
- Ciabatta Buns

Divide the beef into four equal patties, and generously salt and pepper. In pan or on grill, cook them for about 4 to 5 minutes, then flip for another 2 to 3 minutes.

Cut your buns, and butter and toast them.

Starting with the bottom bun, add Siracha Mayo, a few sprigs of cilantro, then the burger patty, and then the pickled vegetables and jalapeño. Finally, add the top bun.

SRIRACHA MAYO

- 1 cup mayo
- 1 tablespoon siracha

Mix until fully combined.

QUICK PICKLED VEGGIES

- ½ cup water
- ¼ cup rice vinegar
- ¼ cup sugar
- ½ teaspoon kosher salt
- 1 large carrot, julienned (thin strips)
- ¼ pound daikon radish, julienned (thin strips)

In a pot, bring the first four ingredients to boil. Remove from heat, then pour over the carrots and daikon. Let cool, then refrigerate.

PULLMAN BREAD

This is probably the most challenging recipe in this book. You'll also need a very specific piece of equipment, a Pullman loaf pan (find it online). This style of bread was used on trains, because the square loaves needed less storage space than round-topped loaves in the compact kitchens of railroad cars.

NOTE: You can use a regular bread pan, but it won't come out with four even crusts.

Prep time: over-night rise for starter, plus about 4-5 hours for dough

Bake time: 40 minutes

Makes 1 loaf

To Make This Bun

Starter

- ¼ cup bread flour
- A pinch active dry yeast
- A pinch salt
- 1 teaspoon sugar
- 3 tablespoons cold milk

Dough

- 3½ cups bread flour
- ¼ cup sugar
- 1 teaspoon salt
- 2 teaspoons active dry yeast
- 1¼ cup cold milk
- 4 eggs
- 8 tablespoons unsalted butter, room temperature

Make the Starter

The night before, in a small bowl, mix the starter ingredients into a paste. Cover with a towel, and leave on the counter. In the morning it'll be puffy and ready to go!

Make the Bread

In a large bowl, add the milk, then the puffy starter. With your fingers, break apart the starter as best you can. Add the flour, salt, yeast, and eggs. Stir with your hand (it works best!) or use a big spoon until it all comes together. It'll be very sticky.

Sprinkle some flour on a board, and scrape the dough onto the floured surface. Knead the dough for about 5 minutes, until it gets smoother, and stops sticking. Form it into a ball, cover with a towel, and let sit for about 15 minutes.

On the same lightly floured surface, take the ball and gently stretch it out into a big rectangle (about twelve by ten inches). Frost the surface of the dough with 7 tablespoons of butter. It doesn't have to cover it perfectly, and doesn't need to look pretty. Fold the dough in thirds, like a sheet of paper being folded to fit an envelope, with one third folded in, and the last third folded over the first, so that the buttered surface is inside. Now take the ends and fold them similarly in thirds, so that you roughly have a ball again. Place the ball back in the bowl and cover with a towel. Let rise for 45–60 minutes.

On same lightly floured surface, take the ball and gently stretch it out again. Refold it the same way you did the before. Place the ball back in the bowl, and cover with a towel. Let rise for 45–60 minutes.

Okay, now a third time, repeating the instructions in the last paragraph.

Generously butter the inside of the loaf pan.

Dust your work surface one last time, and do one more stretching. Fold it again like a letter, but this time, just fold the ends under, so no seams are showing. Carefully lift it and place the dough into buttered pan, seam side down. Make sure the edges are all tucked under. Spread a little butter on top, and slide the lid on.

Your final rise can be anywhere from 2 to 4 hours. Keep an eye on it. When the dough is about a half inch from the lid, you are ready to go.

Preheat the oven to 375 degrees.

NOTE: Place a rimmed baking sheet on the lower rack to catch any butter that drips out!

Bake the loaf for 30 minutes, with the lid on, rotating the pan halfway through.

Remove from oven, take the loaf out of the pan (careful, it's hot!), and place the loaf in the oven for 7 minutes more.

Let cool before slicing.

PULLMAN PATTY MELT

Prep time:
15 minutes to cook and assemble

Makes 4 burgers

To Make This Burger

- 1 pound ground beef
- Swiss cheese
- Caramelized Onion, Pepper, Mushroom sauté
- Mayo
- Salt and pepper
- Pullman bread (or any good toasting bread)

Divide the beef into four equal patties, and generously salt and pepper. In pan or on grill, cook them for about 4 to 5 minutes, then flip, add a slice of Swiss cheese, and cook for another 2 to 3 minutes.

Slice a thick piece of Pullman Bread (store-bought Texas Toast or brioche also works well). Toast in a toaster, or lightly butter and cook in a pan the way you would make a grilled cheese sandwich.

When the cheese is melted, remove the burgers.

Starting with the toast (or grilled bread), add a scoop of the onion/pepper/mushroom mix, and then the burger patty with melted cheese.

A more indulgent version would be a full sandwich, using two pieces of grilled bread.

CARAMELIZED ONION, PEPPER, MUSHROOM SAUTÉ

- 1 tablespoon olive oil
- 1 clove garlic, smashed and chopped
- 2 tablespoons caramelized onions
- 1 red bell pepper (or 1 cup chopped roasted red peppers from a jar)
- 1 cup thinly sliced cremini mushrooms
- 1 tablespoon fresh thyme (or rosemary)

Heat the oil, and cook the garlic for a minute, then add the onions, peppers, and mushrooms, and cook until soft. Add the thyme, and salt and pepper to taste.

MINI CINNAMON BUNS

The cinnamon and sugar on these buns will take you back to your childhood, when you ate cinnamon toast for breakfast. Also try them filled with strawberries and whipped cream, for a unique take on strawberry shortcake.

Prep time: 20 minutes plus about 1.5 hours to proof

Bake time: 25-30 minutes

Makes 16 buns

To Make This Bun

- ⅓ cup bread flour
- ¾ cup water
- 2½ cups bread flour
- 1 tablespoon white sugar
- 1 tablespoon cinnamon
- 2 teaspoons active dry yeast
- 1 teaspoon sea salt
- 1 egg
- ½ cup milk
- ¼ cup softened butter
- 1 egg yolk (for egg wash)
- 3 tablespoons of a mixture of equal parts sugar & cinnamon

In a small saucepan over medium heat, whisk the initial bread flour and the water (the first two ingredients) until they become a smooth, thick paste. Let cool for a bit.

Get out your electric mixer with a dough hook. In the bowl, mix the next four dry ingredients together. In a separate bowl, whisk the egg and milk together. On low speed, slowly add this egg/milk mixture, and then add the paste you made earlier.

Mix on medium speed for 5 minutes. Break apart the softened butter into clumps, and toss them into the mixer as it's running. Mix for an additional 3 minutes. The dough will look smooth but will be super sticky.

Scoop the dough into a lightly oiled bowl. Move the dough ball around until it's oiled all over, then cover with a towel for about 1 hour.

When the dough is big and puffy, it's time to make the buns. Dump the dough out onto a cutting board. It'll deflate, but don't worry, the yeast is still working for you. Divide the dough into sixteen pieces. Do your best to roll each piece of sticky dough into a smooth ball. It helps to fold the dough over itself, so that the top side of the ball has a tight smooth surface.

Preheat oven to 325 degrees.

Place on two parchment lined baking sheets, four per sheet. (This is just for looks. I like a bun that hasn't baked in contact with another bun. You can space them all out on one sheet, but they may rise into each other.) Lightly brush each bun with egg yolk (mix a yolk with a few drops of water), then generously sprinkle them with the cinnamon sugar mixture. Let rise for about 20 minutes.

Bake at 325 degrees for 25–30 minutes, or until the tops start to brown. Let cool on wire racks.

ICE CREAM DESSERT BURGERS

These little guys are a great way to finish any meal. The ice cream and the buns aren't too sweet, and they are just the right size after a big burger. The soft serve is a slightly modified recipe by Justin Chapple from *Food & Wine* magazine. It's lightly sweetened and super creamy, and a pinch to make. No ice cream maker needed.

Prep time:
5 minutes to assemble, but allow additional time to prepare and freeze the ice-cream

Makes 4 burgers

To Make This Burger

- Three Ingredient Soft Serve
- 8 mint leaves
- Mini cinnamon buns

Starting with the bottom bun, place one mint leaf so that it is sticking halfway out of the bun. Then add a scoop of soft serve, and finally add the top bun.

THREE INGREDIENT SOFT SERVE

- 1 pound bag frozen strawberries (or blueberries)
- 1 can sweetened condensed milk
- 1 teaspoon vanilla extract

Let the berries thaw for about 20 minutes. In blender, combine semi thawed berries, condensed milk, and vanilla, and blend until smooth. This is difficult even for a good blender, so go easy, so you don't over-heat the motor. Pour the resulting smoothie mix into a container and freeze.

AND FINALLY, THE ROWAN BERGER

Along with the inspiring burger recipes I've shared with you in this book, here is one more that I cook just for my kid. How could I not include it?

Prep time:
1 minute to assemble

Makes 1 burger

To Make This Burger

- 1 plain burger
- 1 plain bun

Cook burger patty, and toast bun. Add no seeds.

Starting with the bottom bun, add the burger patty (and nothing else). Finally, add the top bun.

ACKNOWLEDGMENTS

I'd love to thank each and every person who has helped me along the way, but the list would be too long.

I want to give a special thanks to my wife Lori and son Rowan, who put up with me as I frantically tried to write a cookbook without any knowledge of how to write a cookbook. They endured way too many burger nights where they ate while I ran around like a madman trying to take the perfect photos of their food. May you never have to eat a burger again!

Thank you to my mom and dad, who have always believed in me and encouraged me to follow my dreams. And to my brothers who probably wouldn't eat any of these burgers.

Special thanks to my friend Rodney Blackwell, who's love of burgers reaches far and wide. Your encouragement of this book and the buns helped get this thing moving, and I can't thank you enough!

Thank you to all the chefs and local food folks who have offered guidance and encouragement through this: Eric V. Miller, Jay Cuff, Michael Tuohy, Hank Shaw, Chris Barnum-Dann, Adam Pechal, Pajo Bruich, David Kaisel and Carolyn Kumpe.

Special thanks to my team at Mango Publishing, who have guided me through this process and put up with all my questions.

And lastly, I want to thank each and every one of you who purchased my book and tried these recipe. It means the world to me.

ABOUT THE AUTHOR

Born and raised in Ohio, Greg moved West first to Chicago then to San Francisco, before settling in Sacramento. He owns a design studio in Sacramento called Pomegranate Design that focuses on graphic design for non-profits and the restaurant industry. After reading a book about sourdough bread, he took up baking as a hobby. Since then, baking has become a passion and a side hustle. He has won blue ribbons for the past 45 years for his breads at the California State Fair, has created bread recipes for some of Sacramento's top restaurants and usually has some buns on hand if anyone wants any.

Mango Publishing, established in 2014, publishes an eclectic list of books by diverse authors—both new and established voices—on topics ranging from business, personal growth, women's empowerment, LGBTQ studies, health, and spirituality to history, popular culture, time management, decluttering, lifestyle, mental wellness, aging, and sustainable living. We were recently named 2019's #1 fastest growing independent publisher by Publishers Weekly. Our success is driven by our main goal, which is to publish high quality books that will entertain readers as well as make a positive difference in their lives.

Our readers are our most important resource; we value your input, suggestions, and ideas. We'd love to hear from you—after all, we are publishing books for you!

Please stay in touch with us and follow us at:

Facebook: Mango Publishing

Twitter: @MangoPublishing

Instagram: @MangoPublishing

LinkedIn: Mango Publishing

Pinterest: Mango Publishing

Sign up for our newsletter at www.mango.bz and receive a free book!

Join us on Mango's journey to reinvent publishing, one book at a time.